THE
Torani
COOKBOOK

Pat,
We hope you
enjoy creating
with Torani,

Pat,
Buon Appetto!

THE *Torani* COOKBOOK

NEW RECIPES WITH THE ORIGINAL ITALIAN SYRUPS

by
Lisa Lucheta
and Ann Rudorf

TEN SPEED PRESS
Berkeley, California

For Ezilda, Rinaldo, and Bunny

❖

A Kirsty Melville book

1O

Ten Speed Press
P.O. Box 7123
Berkeley, CA 94707

Distributed in Australia by E. J. Dwyer Pty Ltd; in Canada by Publishers Group West; in New Zealand by Tandem Press; in South Africa by Real Books; and in the United Kingdom and Europe by Airlift Books.

Cover design by Triad, Inc. and Nancy Austin
Food photography and front cover photograph by Brent Lindstrom
Text design by Triad, Inc. and Catherine Jacobes
Text composition by Catherine Jacobes
Chapter introduction photography by Jean Lannon
Photographs on pages viii and xii by Mark Hundley
Food styling by Randy Mon
Additional writing by Richard Kauffman

Library of Congress Cataloging in Publication Data
Lucheta, Lisa.
     The Torani cookbook/ by Lisa Lucheta.
        p. cm.
     Includes index.
     ISBN 0-89815-803-6
     I. Cookery (Syrups) I. Title.
     TX819.S96L83 1996
     641.6'36—dc20
                                      95-39486
                                      CIP

Printed in Malaysia

I 2 3 4 5 — 00 99 98 97 96

PREFACE

WHEN I WAS TEN YEARS OLD, my brother Paul and I would go to work with my father during summer vacation. I remember the great smells of sugar and fruit as Torani syrups were being blended and bottled. Sometimes we "helped" Leonard Robbs label the bottles, taking them from his hand after the machine glued the label and placing them back on the long wooden tables where they waited to be cased. When we passed a cafe in North Beach and saw the row of Torani bottles behind the counter, I'd say to my brother, "I wonder if we labeled any of those." Later, when Paul and I were at college in Berkeley, we saw the Torani "banner" of flavors every day in cafes all over town.

I still feel the same sense of pride whenever I see Torani in a cafe or on a store shelf. Our facilities are more automated now, but we've managed to maintain our standards of quality, our sense of family, and—most important—our enjoyment of what we're doing.

This book has been a proud labor of love for us. Although our Chef and Culinary Director Ann Rudorf and I receive authorship credit, *The Torani Cookbook* is the collaborative work of many people in our larger Torani family. In recognition of this, several voices are represented in the introduction to each of the five chapters of recipes in the book.

We wish to thank those who have worked with R. Torre & Company, whose commitment, passion, and talent ensure that every concept exceeds expectations. We greatly appreciate the inspiration of our loyal and innovative customers and the energy and ideas of those who have helped promote us in the marketplace.

Special thanks to: my father Harry and my brother Paul for embracing the qualities that are at the heart of Torani—the sense of tradition, adherence to excellence, and a creative eye toward the far horizon; Melanie Dulbecco, for spearheading this enormous project from concept to completion, for determining and executing its artistic direction, for hours of editing, and as ever, for leading the team; Ann Rudorf, for her superb palate, creativity, and judicious ingredient selection—many thanks for her endless hours of recipe development and tasting, for her avid interest in the project, and for ushering in the new era of culinary applications for Torani syrups; Brandy Brandenburger, a pioneer in an uncharted category, for his brilliant vision fifteen years ago of *caffè lattes* floating with Torani syrups; Matt Brandenburger, for his coffee expertise, his industry knowledge, and his unyielding desire to export Torani to the world; Becky Fyffe, marketing wizard, for hours of recipe development and editing; and Domenico Milano, "Il Dottore," for his exceptional ability to combine ingredients and for his energetic dedication to excellence.

America's cuisine is a grand palette, full of ever-changing possibilities. We are delighted to offer our contribution to it.

CONTENTS

THE FIRST AMERICAN Revolution began with tea in Boston. Another, more than 200 years later, began with coffee in Seattle.

In the early 1980s, strong, rich, whole-bean coffees started to challenge the traditional American "cup of Joe." This movement spawned a new kind of coffee house, one designed around a gleaming espresso machine. Italian-style cafes began appearing on downtown streets, in malls, and in bookstores.

Aiding this coffee coup d'état was a product many people recognized by its colorful label and vibrant flavors—Torani Italian Syrups. These fruit-, nut-, and spice-based flavorings,

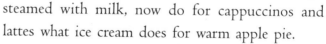

steamed with milk, now do for cappuccinos and lattes what ice cream does for warm apple pie.

Syrups made from fruit extracts have a long history in Europe, where recipes are often a source of family pride. Processes vary from region to region, but invariably the best syrups are made with fine natural ingredients and loving attention to detail. For generations, Italians have combined natural fruit syrups with sparkling water to make Italian sodas, which were perhaps the world's first soft drinks—and as flavorful and refreshing as anything on the market today.

In 1925, Rinaldo Torre returned to San Francisco from a visit to Lucca, Italy, with several recipes; and so began the production of Italian flavoring syrups in America.

With his wife Ezilda, Rinaldo set up shop in North Beach, San Francisco's burgeoning Italian community. In the back of their wholesale grocery, they boiled and pressed fruit, nuts, and spices, blended the concentrated extracts with pure cane sugar and water in large redwood vats, and fine-tuned the flavor until it tasted just like the syrups of Lucca. Five Torani syrups—Lemon, Grenadine, Tamarindo, Orgeat (Almond), and Anisette—soon became a staple in local cafes and specialty grocery stores. For the Italians in North Beach, it was a welcome touch of home.

Ezilda (right) and her sister Evelyn near their North Beach home, 1910

When Rinaldo died in 1938, Ezilda took over the operation of R. Torre & Company. In 1955, the Torres' son-in-law, Harry Lucheta, joined the enterprise and successfully expanded the line of syrups and their market. (A third generation, Lisa and Paul Lucheta, has since taken up the family tradition.) By the late 1970s, twenty-five flavors could be found in Italian restaurants, cafes, and specialty stores throughout California. Then the espresso revolution was sparked.

THE CAPPUCCINO TASTED 'ROUND THE WORLD

L. C. "Brandy" Brandenburger, a coffee-industry veteran and entrepreneur from Portland, Oregon, was having a cappuccino one day in the landmark Caffe Trieste in North Beach. He noticed a row of brightly colored bottles behind the bar and asked the owner what they were. He ordered an Italian soda, liked it, and took a few bottles of Torani home to Portland.

Brandy began experimenting by adding the syrups to cappuccinos and lattes he made on his home espresso machine. His first concoction, Orange Fantasia, was Torani Orange syrup steamed with milk, added to espresso and dusted with nutmeg. From the first taste, he knew he was on to something big.

Brandy started contacting coffee distributors and cafe owners he knew from his thirty years in the coffee business. At first they thought he was crazy. "You put *what* in your cappuccino?" they would ask. But he persisted, carrying his message to cafes in Seattle, San Francisco, and New York. He expanded his repertoire of drinks, wrote down the recipes, and passed them out to his customers. Gradually the idea caught on. Then it took off.

Since then, people in cafes nationwide have had a lot of fun dreaming up—and enjoying—new Torani espresso drinks. The first chapter of this book is full of their creations and Brandy's. We invented some of our own, too, from Raspberry Truffle Latte to Roca® Mocha to Hot Apple Pie Steamer. With our quick tips for steaming syrups with milk, you will soon be making the perfect flavored espresso drinks at home.

General store, Lucca, Italy

Next up, a trip home to North Beach, and even back to Lucca. Classic sodas and Italian ices join with freezes, flavored teas, and smoothies, inviting you to enjoy the refreshing drinks for which these syrups were first made. Dozens of twists on old classics such as Cream Soda, as well as enticing new recipes such as Mango Smoothie, await. Once you have the basics, your imagination can run free—perhaps a vanilla frozen yogurt smoothie flavored with Irish cream or a glass of ice-cold tea refreshed with boysenberry.

The next three chapters take our revolution in flavor a step further. A few years ago, we asked ourselves, "If the syrups can flavor hot and cold drinks so successfully, why not food?" So we brought in chef Ann Rudorf to start investigating.

We were delighted with the outcome. The syrups adapted

wonderfully to new uses—marinades and muffins alike. From yams baked with a touch of praline to homemade waffles flavored with English toffee, Ann found Torani syrups versatile, easy to use, and positively inspiring. As a chef, Ann appreciated above all that Torani's flavors were consistently true, however the syrups were used. Dependable quality has everything to do with how we blend our syrups.

FLAVORS WORTH FIGHTING FOR

Through the development of nearly fifty flavors (see page 129), we've remained faithful to Rinaldo's basic recipe for producing high-quality syrups—the very best ingredients and a great deal of care. We frequently begin by com-bining several natural extracts from a variety of sources around the world: a raspberry extract from France will not taste the same as one from New York, so we blend them and experiment. After we've achieved the right balance, we test the syrup in every appropriate application—it has to be able to withstand heat and cold without losing its flavor. We adjust the recipe and repeat the process until we're satisfied. A syrup can take up to a year to develop, but when it's done, it is delicious and wonderfully versatile.

The results of Ann's collaboration with us fill this book—drinks, salsas, marinades, desserts, entrées, side dishes, and more. At first, we provided these recipes only to distributors, cafes, and stores that sold Torani syrups. But their response was so terrific, we wanted to share them with you. We hope they inspire you to experiment with Torani syrups and create your own sensational drinks and dishes. When you do, please send your recipes to us—we'd love to try them.

CAFFE LATTES, CAPPUCCINOS, MOCHAS, AND STEAMERS

WHAT I LOVE ABOUT THESE DRINKS is that they're completely handmade. There's nothing automated or mass produced about a flavored cappuccino.

The whole process of making the perfect espresso drink or steamer rests on two things: top quality ingredients and a skilled individual at the controls. In cafes this person is called a *barista*. Good baristas know everything about espresso—where the beans are grown, how they're roasted, how to grind them, and how to store them. They know how to steam milk to the right temperature and how much syrup to use in a flavored drink. One barista might prefer espresso beans grown in Costa Rica, while another will use beans grown in Indonesia. And each barista has an individual style. A hazelnut latte won't be exactly the same from one cafe to the next. Many of us with espresso machines at home now make great tasting mochas and cappuccinos.

Espresso drinks have come a long way in a very short time. When I started promoting the idea of using flavoring syrups in lattes and cappuccinos, you could find three espresso machines in all of Seattle. I experimented with all of the Torani syrups available and tried them with my son Matt. Like anything worthwhile, the basic recipes took some time and tinkering to perfect, but when we served them to our customers and to cafe owners—magic.

Many of the recipes you'll find in this chapter are based on the original ones I invented in my kitchen. Others are the creations of baristas from around the country. Try them, then try your own—you'll be amazed what you can do with fine coffee, fresh milk, and Torani syrups.

Brandy Brandenburger

Coffee Industry Consultant
Inventor of the flavored latte

Espresso Basics

The following are definitions of traditional coffee drinks savored by aficionados everywhere. These are the foundation for the delicious recipes in the following pages.

Espresso

One to one and one-half ounces strong, rich coffee with light brown, creamy foam on top (called *crema*), served in a demitasse cup. Espresso does not designate a specific type of bean. Rather it signifies an efficient method of brewing finely ground coffee under pressure to obtain maximum extraction from the grounds. Properly made, espresso should have excellent flavor with a minimum degree of acidity or bitterness.

Cappuccino

One to one and one-half ounces espresso topped with equal parts of steamed milk and a crown of rich foam. It is usually served in a six-ounce cup.

Caffè Latte

Two to three ounces espresso combined with eight ounces steamed milk and topped with a crown of rich foam. It is served in a twelve- to sixteen-ounce glass.

❖

The government of a nation is often decided over a cup of coffee.

—CARDINAL RICHELIEU

❖

CAFFÈ LATTES AND CAPPUCCINOS

Americans give a new twist to the traditional espresso drinks by adding flavors. A regular latte or cappuccino takes on a new identity with a splash of hazelnut or vanilla.

We start with the Torani classics below, then progress to creative improvisations. Don't hesitate to substitute any other flavors if the mood strikes you. These are just the beginning.

HOW MUCH SYRUP SHOULD I ADD?

Here are general guidelines for measuring how much syrup to add to a latte or cappuccino. However, please feel free to throw out all the rules and add as much or as little syrup as you find personally pleasing.

6-ounce cup = 1/4 to 1/2 ounce

8-ounce cup = 1/2 ounce

12-ounce cup = 3/4 ounce

16-ounce cup = 1 ounce

CLASSIC TORANI LATTE

- 2 ounces hot espresso
- $3/_4$ ounce Vanilla syrup
- 4 to 6 ounces cold milk
- Ground cinnamon or cocoa, for dusting

Pour the espresso into a 12-ounce glass. Steam the syrup and milk and pour into a glass, allowing the espresso and the densely foamed milk to fold together. Dust the top with cinnamon or cocoa powder.

Note: While Vanilla has always been a popular classic, other favorites used for this drink include Orgeat (Almond) and Hazelnut.

CLASSIC TORANI CAPPUCCINO

- 2 ounces cold milk
- 2 ounces hot espresso
- $\frac{1}{4}$ to $\frac{1}{2}$ ounce Orgeat (Almond) syrup
- Cocoa or ground nutmeg, for dusting

Steam the syrup and milk together and allow to sit while you prepare your espresso. Pour the espresso into a 6-ounce cup. Gently add the hot, steamed milk until the cup is about two-thirds full. Spoon the light foam over the top of the beverage to form a peak and dust with cocoa or nutmeg.

CLASSIC ICED TORANI LATTE

- Ice
- 2 ounces espresso
- 1 ounce Irish Cream or other Torani syrup
- 8 ounces cold milk
- Whipped cream, for topping
- Shaved chocolate, for topping

Fill a 16-ounce glass with ice. Add the espresso and the syrup. Pour in the milk and stir. Top with whipped cream and shaved chocolate for true decadence.

STEAMING MILK AND SYRUP TOGETHER

For best results, we recommend that you steam your favorite syrup flavors and cold milk together in a pitcher before you add them to the beverage. This brings out the full body and aroma of the flavor. If you prefer to steam the milk without the syrup, be sure to add the syrup to the cup first, then the espresso, then the steamed milk, and stir.

RASPBERRY LAYERED LATTE

- *2 to 3 ounces hot espresso*
- *1 ounce Raspberry syrup*
- *4 ounces cold milk*
- *Vanilla powder, for dusting*
- *Ground cinnamon, for dusting*

Steam the syrup and milk together and pour the densely steamed milk into a 12-ounce glass, until the glass is about two-thirds full. Gently pour (or spoon) the lightly foamed milk on top to about 1 inch below the lip of the glass. Slowly pour the espresso through the middle of the foam peak. The espresso will form a rich, dark layer between the layers of milk. Dust with vanilla and cinnamon. (Pictured opposite.)

❖

MILK EXPANDS WHEN STEAMED

Steamed properly, milk expands to as much as twice its original volume. Therefore 4 ounces of cold milk should render 8 ounces of steamed milk. Depending on your particular espresso machine, you may need 4 to 6 ounces of cold milk to produce 8 ounces of steamed milk.

❖

ROCA® PEEL LATTE

Thanks to Ian Goodman of the Blink Cafe in Lookout Mountain, Georgia for this delicious recipe.

- *2 ounces hot espresso*
- *³/₄ ounce Almond Roca® syrup*
- *³/₄ ounce Mandarin Orange syrup*
- *4 to 6 ounces cold milk*
- *Sliced almonds, for garnish*
- *Twist of orange peel, for garnish*

Pour the espresso into a 12-ounce glass. Steam the syrups and milk together and add to the glass. Garnish with the almonds and orange peel.

CAFFE NIKKO CAPPUCCINO

- *1/3 ounce Mandarin Orange syrup*
- *1/8 ounce Creme de Cacao syrup*
- *2 ounces cold milk*
- *1 1/2 ounces hot espresso*
- *Cocoa, for dusting*
- *Sugared orange peel, for garnish*

Steam the syrups and milk together and allow to sit while preparing the espresso. Pour the espresso into a 6-ounce cup. Gently add the steamed milk, topping the beverage with a rich crown of foam. Dust with cocoa and garnish with sugared orange peel.

DREAM CREAM LATTE

- *2 to 3 ounces hot espresso*
- *1/3 ounce Mandarin Orange syrup*
- *1/3 ounce Vanilla syrup*
- *4 ounces cold milk*
- *Cocoa, for dusting*
- *Shaved coconut, for garnish*

Pour the espresso into a 12-ounce glass. Steam the syrup and milk together and add to the glass. Dust with cocoa and garnish with shaved coconut.

CARAMEL APPLE LATTE

- *2 to 3 ounces hot espresso*
- *1/2 to 3/4 ounce Caramel syrup*
- *1/4 to 1/2 ounce Apple syrup*
- *4 to 6 ounces cold milk*
- *Ground cinnamon, for dusting*
- *Slice of apple, for garnish*

Pour the espresso into a 16-ounce glass. Steam the syrup and milk together and add to the glass. Dust with cinnamon and garnish with a slice of apple.

PREHEAT YOUR CUP

For a better beverage with more staying power, preheat your cup or glass with hot water before introducing the beverage.

LAVA FLOW

Thanks to Philip Price Engle of Espresso Bravissimo Coffee in Honolulu, Hawaii for this creative recipe.

- *½ ounce sweetened condensed milk*
- *½ ounce chocolate syrup*
- *2 ounces hot espresso*
- *Ice*
- *8 ounces cold milk*
- *Whipped cream, for topping*
- *½ ounce Raspberry syrup*

Pour the condensed milk, chocolate syrup, and espresso into a 12-ounce glass and stir. Fill the glass with ice and pour in the milk. Top with whipped cream and drizzle the Raspberry syrup through the middle and around the sides. Ooh, the goddess Pele is pleased!

B-52 LATTE

- *2 ounces hot espresso*
- *⅓ ounce Irish Cream syrup*
- *⅓ ounce Coffee syrup*
- *⅛ ounce Mandarin Orange syrup*
- *4 to 6 ounces cold milk*

Pour the espresso into a 12-ounce glass. Steam the syrups and milk together and add to the glass. This is a great nonalcoholic twist on an old bar favorite.

RASPBERRY TRUFFLE LATTE

- *2 to 3 ounces hot espresso*
- *½ ounce Raspberry syrup*
- *¼ ounce Creme de Cacao syrup*
- *4 to 6 ounces cold milk*
- *Cocoa, for dusting*

Pour the espresso into a 12-ounce glass. Steam the syrups and milk together and add to the glass. Dust with cocoa.

Ice Caffè Amoré

Thanks to Suzanne Cruzen of Cruzen a Latte in Vancouver, Washington for this recipe idea.

❖

PUT IT ON ICE

All of your favorite latte and cappuccino recipes may be made iced. It's as simple as substituting chilled milk for steamed milk.

❖

- *Ice*
- *2 ounces espresso*
- *1 ounce Tiramisu syrup*
- *¹/₈ ounce Mandarin Orange syrup*
- *8 ounces cold milk*

Fill a 16-ounce glass with ice. Add the espresso, syrups, and milk and stir.

Variation: For a creamier note, top with half-and-half.

Cherry Cheesecake Latte

Thanks to Donna Slinger of Java Joe's Espresso in Norfolk, Virginia for this rich recipe. It's also great iced.

- *2 ounces hot espresso*
- *¹/₂ ounce Irish Cream syrup*
- *¹/₂ ounce Cherry syrup*
- *¹/₈ ounce Vanilla syrup*
- *Dash of Orgeat (Almond) syrup*
- *4 to 6 ounces cold milk*

Pour the espresso into a 12-ounce glass. Steam the syrups and milk together and add to the glass.

Variation: Raspberry or Strawberry may be substituted for Cherry.

Coco Mocho

- *2 ounces hot espresso*
- *¹⁄₈ ounce Coconut syrup*
- *¹⁄₈ ounce Creme de Cacao syrup*
- *4 to 6 ounces cold milk*
- *Cocoa, for dusting*
- *Shaved coconut, for topping*

Pour the espresso into a
12-ounce glass. Steam the syrup
and milk together and add to
the glass. Dust with cocoa and
top with shaved coconut.

Hazelnut Decadence

- *2 ounces hot espresso*
- *¹⁄₂ ounce Hazelnut syrup*
- *¹⁄₂ ounce Creme de Cacao syrup*
- *4 to 6 ounces cold milk*
- *Cocoa, for dusting*

Pour the espresso into a
12-ounce glass. Steam the
syrups and milk together and
add to the glass. Dust with
cocoa and Hazelnut syrup.

STEAMING TIP

To achieve beautiful, dense
foam without scalding the
milk, we recommend chilling
the steaming pitcher
prior to use.

Nothing *warms the senses so much as a velvety mocha. One of the most popular drinks in cafes, mochas are a mixture of espresso, chocolate, and steamed milk that is topped with whipped cream. A dash of flavor adds extra richness.*

❖

Chocolate flatters you for a while. It warms you for an instant; then, all of a sudden, it kindles a mortal fever in you.

—MADAME DE SÉVIGNÉ
IN A LETTER TO
HER DAUGHTER

❖

TURTLE MOCHA

- *2 ounces hot espresso*
- *$1/3$ ounce Caramel syrup*
- *Splash of Praline syrup*
- *1 tablespoon cocoa*
- *4 to 6 ounces cold milk*
- *Chocolate sprinkles, for topping*

Pour the espresso into a 12-ounce glass. Steam the syrups, cocoa, and milk together and add to the glass. Top with extra cocoa and chocolate sprinkles.

ORANGE VANILLA MOCHA

Thanks to Joshua Crow of Cafe D'Arte in Seattle, Washington for this creamy recipe.

- *1 ounce chocolate syrup*
- *$1/2$ ounce Vanilla syrup*
- *$1/2$ ounce Mandarin Orange syrup*
- *4 to 6 ounces cold milk*
- *2 ounces hot espresso*

Pour the syrups into a 12-ounce glass. Steam the Mandarin Orange syrup and milk together and allow to sit. Add the espresso to the mixture in the glass and stir. Pour in the flavored steamed milk.

RASPBERRY MOCHA

- *2 ounces hot espresso*
- *³/₄ ounce chocolate syrup*
- *¹/₂ ounce Raspberry syrup*
- *4 to 6 ounces cold milk*
- *Cocoa, for dusting*
- *Chocolate sprinkles, for topping*

Pour the espresso into a 12-ounce glass. Steam the syrups and milk together and add to the glass. Dust with cocoa and top with chocolate sprinkles.

ICED ALMOND MOCHA

- *2 ounces espresso*
- *Ice*
- *³/₄ ounce chocolate syrup*
- *¹/₂ ounce Orgeat (Almond) syrup*
- *8 ounces cold milk*
- *Almond-flavored whipped cream (page 17), for topping*
- *Cocoa, for dusting*
- *Sliced almonds, for garnish*

Pour the espresso into a 12-ounce glass filled with ice. Add the syrups and milk, and stir. Top with the whipped cream, dust with the cocoa, and garnish with the sliced almonds.

ICED BLACK FOREST MOCHA

- 2 ounces espresso
- Ice
- 1/2 ounce chocolate syrup
- 1/4 ounce Cherry syrup
- 1/4 ounce Coconut syrup
- 8 ounces cold milk
- Whipped cream, for topping
- Shaved chocolate, for topping
- 1 Bing cherry, for garnish

Pour the espresso into a 12-ounce glass filled with ice. Add the syrups and milk and stir. Top with a generous dollop of whipped cream, the shaved chocolate, and garnish with the cherry. (Pictured opposite.)

MAKE THAT MOCHA A LATTE

If you'd like your mocha a little less sweet and more like a latte, substitute Creme de Cacao syrup for chocolate syrup.

DOUBLE DECADENCE DELIGHT

Thanks to Jake Gordon of Austin Chase in Seattle, Washington for this delicious recipe.

- 8 ounces cold milk
- Ice
- 2 ounces espresso
- 1 ounce chocolate syrup
- 1 ounce Caramel syrup
- Whipped cream, for topping
- Finely chopped walnuts, for garnish

Pour the milk into a 16-ounce glass filled with ice. Add espresso and syrup and stir. Top with the whipped cream and garnish with drizzled chocolate or Caramel syrup (or both) and chopped walnuts.

ROCA® MOCHA

- ½ ounce chocolate syrup
- ¾ ounce Almond Roca® syrup
- 2 ounces espresso
- 8 ounces steamed milk
- Whipped cream, for topping
- 1 Almond Roca® candy, crumbled, for garnish

Pour the syrups and espresso into a 12-ounce glass and stir. Add the steamed milk to 1 inch from the top of the glass. Swirl on the whipped cream and sprinkle with the crumbled candy.

CHOCO-TOFFEE COFFEE

- 2 ounces hot espresso
- ½ ounce chocolate syrup
- ½ ounce English Toffee syrup
- 4 to 6 ounces cold milk
- Whipped cream, for topping
- Toffee bar, crumbled, for garnish

Pour the espresso into a 12-ounce glass. Steam the syrups and milk together and add to the glass. Top with whipped cream and crushed toffee bar.

NIGHT IN VENICE

- 2 ounces hot espresso
- ½ ounce chocolate syrup
- ½ ounce Amaretto syrup
- ½ ounce Cherry syrup
- 4 to 6 ounces cold milk
- Amaretto-flavored whipped cream (page 17), for topping

Pour the espresso into a 12-ounce glass. Steam the syrups and milk together and add to the glass. Top with the whipped cream.

MOCHA ROYALE

- *2 ounces hot espresso*
- *³/₄ ounce chocolate syrup*
- *¹/₂ ounce Vanilla syrup*
- *4 to 6 ounces cold milk*
- *Whipped cream, for topping*
- *Vanilla powder, for dusting*
- *Chocolate-covered espresso bean, for garnish*

Pour the espresso into a 12-ounce glass. Steam the syrups and milk together and add to the glass. Swirl on some whipped cream, dust with the vanilla powder, and garnish with the espresso bean.

FLAVORED WHIPPED CREAM

Flavored whipped cream on top of a beverage or dessert can be a real show stopper, and it's easy to do. Blend together 1 cup chilled whipping cream and 3 to 4 tablespoons of your favorite Torani syrup. (Vanilla or Raspberry is always a hit.) Beat the syrup and chilled cream until firm peaks are held.

PECAN PIE MOCHA

- *2 ounces hot espresso*
- *³/₄ ounce chocolate syrup*
- *¹/₂ ounce Praline syrup*
- *¹/₄ ounce Toasted Walnut syrup*
- *Splash of Caramel syrup*
- *4 to 6 ounces cold milk*
- *Vanilla-flavored whipped cream (see sidebar), for topping*
- *1 pecan half, for garnish*

Pour the espresso into a 12-ounce glass. Steam the syrups and milk together and add to the glass. Top with the whipped cream and the pecan half.

STEAMERS

For those who like to tickle their taste buds without espresso, steamers are a great alternative. This drink is a combination of milk and syrup steamed together until warm and frothy.

The recipes in the Caffè Lattes and Cappuccino section may be used to make steamers by simply eliminating the espresso. Likewise, the recipes here may be used to make caffè lattes by simply adding espresso.

❖

ITALIAN CUSTARD

- ½ ounce Italian Eggnog syrup
- ½ ounce Praline syrup
- 4 to 6 ounces cold milk
- Ground nutmeg, for dusting

Steam the syrups and milk together until warm and frothy. Pour into a 10-ounce glass and dust with nutmeg.

❖

HOT CHOCOLATE BANANA

- ½ ounce Creme de Banana syrup
- ½ ounce chocolate or Creme de Cacao syrup
- 1 teaspoon cocoa
- 4 to 6 ounces cold milk

Steam the syrups, cocoa, and milk together until warm and frothy. Pour into a 10-ounce glass and dust with extra cocoa.

ALOHA STEAMER

- ³/₄ ounce Macadamia Nut syrup
- ¹/₄ ounce Vanilla syrup
- 4 ounces cold milk
- Vanilla powder, for dusting

Steam the syrups and milk together and pour into a 10-ounce glass. Dust with the vanilla powder.

GEORGIA STEAMER

- ³/₄ ounce Peach syrup
- ¹/₄ ounce Apricot syrup
- Splash of Vanilla syrup
- 4 ounces cold milk
- Peach and vanilla flavored whipped cream (page 17), for topping

Steam the syrups and milk together and pour into a 10-ounce glass. Top with the whipped cream.

HOT BUTTERED TOFFEE

- ³/₄ ounce English Toffee syrup
- ¹/₄ ounce Butterscotch syrup
- 4 ounces cold milk
- 1 ounce half-and-half
- Ground nutmeg, for dusting

Steam the syrups, milk, and half-and-half together and pour into a 10-ounce glass. Sprinkle with nutmeg.

GARNISHING HOT ESPRESSO BEVERAGES AND STEAMERS

There's always cocoa, cinnamon, vanilla, nutmeg, and of course, whipped cream. Here are additional, fun ideas: slivered almonds • toasted, chopped nuts • pecan halves • twists of orange or lemon peel • grated orange peel • chocolate-covered espresso beans • shaved white or dark chocolate • shaved coconut • cinnamon sticks • crushed candies • wafer roll cookies • peppermint sticks • colored sprinkles • drizzles of syrup • chocolate dipped fruit

HAZELNUT SUPREMO

- $^3/_4$ ounce Hazelnut syrup
- $^1/_4$ ounce Vanilla syrup
- 3 to 6 ounces cold milk
- Vanilla powder, for dusting
- 1 shaved hazelnut, for garnish

Steam the syrups and milk together and pour into a 10-ounce glass. Dust with vanilla and garnish with the hazelnut. (Pictured opposite.)

HOT APPLE PIE

- $^3/_4$ ounce Apple syrup
- $^1/_4$ ounce Cinnamon syrup
- 4 to 6 ounces cold milk
- Caramel-flavored whipped cream (page 17), for topping
- 1 slice apple, for garnish

Steam the syrups and milk together and pour into a 10-ounce glass. Top with the whipped cream and garnish with the apple slice.

AMARETTO STEAMER

- 1 ounce Amaretto syrup
- 4 ounces cold milk
- Cocoa, for dusting

Steam the syrup and milk together until warm and frothy. Pour into a 10-ounce glass and sprinkle with cocoa.

CHOCOLATE DIPPED FRUIT

A chocolate-dipped strawberry is a perfect accompaniment to a steamer, mocha, or latte. Melt a block of your favorite chocolate in a double boiler (or microwave). Remove from the heat. Dip the strawberries, one by one, gently twirling them in the melted chocolate. Place them on a cookie sheet with parchment paper, and pop in the refrigerator. Allow 10 minutes in the refrigerator for the chocolate to harden. For extra flavor, stir a dash of flavored syrup into the melted chocolate before dipping the fruit.

ITALIAN SODAS, ICED TEAS, SMOOTHIES, AND FREEZES

IF YOU'VE NEVER TASTED an Italian soda, you are missing a real treat. Take some club soda, sparkling water, or seltzer, add some ice, then a splash of Torani Strawberry, Mandarin Orange, or Peach syrup—or any flavor you like. To me, it's what soft drinks were meant to be.

In the early days in North Beach and in the other Italian districts of San Francisco, you found Torani syrups primarily in Italian grocery stores—Rossi's, Molinari's, Lucca's, Genova's. It wasn't until the 1970s that Torani's popularity spread outside the Italian community. University coffee houses started serving Italian sodas, and people began adding the syrups to iced tea and smoothies and concocting all sorts of fabulous drinks.

Freezes, or granitas, are syrup-based ices—like sorbets, but with a coarser texture—and they are another terrific way to use Torani syrups in a traditional Italian mode.

The sodas, freezes, mocktails, and other drinks on the following pages are the result of years of customer creativity. Every week people send us recipes for new drinks they've invented. I've been in the business for forty years, and I'm still amazed by people's inspired ideas.

Harry N. Luchetti

R. Torre & Company

ITALIAN SODAS

The fruity crispness of an Italian soda brightens any afternoon. To enhance the flavor of these sparkling recipes, we suggest that you stir the syrup into the soda and ice. Experimenting with nut and spice flavors is another way to enjoy this authentic Italian delight.

❖

CLASSIC TORANI ITALIAN SODA

Any fruit flavor is perfect for a classic Italian soda. Don't hesitate to put your signature on a traditional recipe. Experiment with combining different flavors to create your own classic.

- 8 ounces sparkling water
- Ice
- 1 to 1 1/2 ounces Raspberry or other flavor of syrup
- Sprig of mint or twist of lemon peel, for garnish

Pour the sparkling water into a 12-ounce glass filled with ice. Add the syrup and stir. Garnish with the mint or lemon peel.

❖

STRAWBERRY TRUFFLE SODA

Serve this drink with fresh strawberries dipped in chocolate (page 21).

- Ice
- 8 ounces sparkling water
- 3/4 ounce Strawberry syrup
- 1/4 ounce Creme de Cacao syrup

Fill a 12-ounce glass with ice and add the sparkling water. Stir in the syrups.

CLASSIC TORANI CREAM SODA

The trick to a successful cream soda is the order of the ingredients. Any flavored syrup can be used to make this luscious drink.

- 1 ounce cold milk
- 1 to 1½ ounces Peach or other flavor of syrup
- Ice
- 8 ounces sparkling water
- Fresh fruit or half-and-half, for garnish

Pour the milk and syrup into a 12-ounce glass. Stir well. Fill the glass with ice, then add sparkling water. Stir again. Garnish with fresh fruit or a teaspoon of half-and-half.

DOUBLE BERRY SODA

- Ice
- 8 ounces sparkling water
- ³/₄ ounce Raspberry syrup
- ¹/₄ ounce Strawberry syrup
- 1 fresh strawberry, for garnish
- 1 flower, for garnish

Fill a 12-ounce glass with ice and add the sparkling water. Stir in the syrups and garnish with a strawberry and a flower.

Variation: For a Triple Berry Soda, add a splash of Blackberry syrup!

PEACHES'N'CREAM

- 1 ounce cold milk
- ³/₄ ounce Peach syrup
- ¹/₄ ounce Vanilla syrup
- Ice
- 8 ounces sparkling water
- Sprig of mint, for garnish

Pour the milk and syrups into a 12-ounce glass. Stir well. Fill the glass with ice and add sparkling water. Stir again. Garnish with the mint.

HOW MUCH SYRUP SHOULD I ADD?

Here are general guidelines for measuring how much syrup to add for Italian sodas. We encourage you to break all the rules, however, and add as much or as little syrup as you like.

6-ounce cup = 1/2 ounce
8-ounce cup = 3/4 ounce
12-ounce cup = 1 ounce
16-ounce cup = 1 1/2 ounces

PINK GRAPEFRUIT SODA

- Ice
- 8 ounces sparkling water
- 2 ounces Pink Grapefruit syrup
- Dash of lemon juice, for topping
- Twist of lemon peel, for garnish

Fill a 12-ounce glass with ice and add the sparkling water. Stir in the syrup. Top with the lemon juice and garnish with the lemon peel. (Pictured opposite.)

CREAMSICLE

- 1 ounce cold milk
- ³/₄ ounce Mandarin Orange syrup
- ¹/₄ ounce Vanilla syrup
- Ice
- 8 ounces sparkling water
- 1 slice orange, for garnish
- 1 teaspoon half-and-half, for floating

Pour the milk and syrup into a 12-ounce glass. Stir well. Fill the glass with ice and add the sparkling water. Stir again. Garnish with the orange slice and float a teaspoon of half-and-half.

WHAT KIND OF WATER?

Seltzer water, club soda, or any kind of plain carbonated water is great with flavoring syrups. Mineral waters are good too, especially those with moderate mineral content. Those with high mineral and salt content may interfere with the flavor of the syrup. Test the syrups in various kinds of carbonated water to find one that is pleasing to you.

MIDNIGHT BRAZILIAN

- Ice
- 8 ounces sparkling water
- ³/₄ ounces Coffee syrup
- ¹/₄ ounce Creme de Cacao syrup
- 1 ounce milk
- Sliver of chocolate, for garnish

Fill a 12-ounce glass with ice and add the sparkling water. Stir in syrups. Garnish with a sliver of chocolate.

SUNRISE SODA

- *Ice*
- *8 ounces sparkling water*
- *³/₄ ounce Mandarin Orange syrup*
- *¹/₄ ounce Pineapple syrup*
- *Slice of pineapple, for garnish*

Fill a 12-ounce glass with ice and add the sparkling water. Stir in the syrup and garnish with the slice of pineapple.

SODA SWAP

Try ginger ale in place of sparkling water for added sweetness and snap. It's especially good with citrus and tropical flavors.

APRICOT KISS

- *Ice*
- *8 ounces sparkling water*
- *³/₄ ounce Apricot syrup*
- *¹/₄ ounce Peach syrup*
- *Sprig of mint, for garnish*

Fill a 12-ounce glass with ice and add the sparkling water. Stir in the syrups and garnish with the mint.

CHERRY-LIME RICKEY

- *Ice*
- *8 ounces sparkling water*
- *¹/₂ to 1 ounce Cherry syrup*
- *¹/₂ to 1 ounce Lime syrup*
- *Slice of lime, for garnish*
- *1 Bing cherry, for garnish*

Fill a tall, 12-ounce chimney glass with ice and add the sparkling water. Stir in the syrups. Garnish with the lime slice and the cherry.

TROPICAL BREEZE

- Ice
- 8 ounces sparkling water
- $1/2$ ounce Creme de Banana syrup
- $1/4$ ounce Pineapple syrup
- $1/4$ ounce Coconut syrup
- Slice of fresh pineapple, for garnish
- Shaved coconut, for garnish

Fill a 12-ounce glass with ice and add the sparkling water. Stir in the syrups. Garnish with the pineapple and shaved coconut.

PINK LEMONADE

Make your regular lemonade "pink" by adding Pink Grapefruit syrup.

GEORGIA MIST

- Ice
- 8 ounces sparkling water
- $1/2$ ounce Apricot syrup
- $1/2$ ounce Lime syrup
- Slice of lime, for garnish

Fill a 12-ounce glass with ice and add the sparkling water. Stir in the syrups and garnish with the lime.

CITRUS SIESTA

- Ice
- 8 ounces sparkling water
- $1/2$ ounce Lemon syrup
- $1/2$ ounce Lime syrup
- Splash of Pink Grapefruit syrup
- Slice of orange, for garnish

Fill a 12-ounce glass with ice and add the sparkling water. Stir in the syrups and garnish with the orange.

ALMOND-MOCHA SODA

- *Ice*
- *8 ounces sparkling water*
- *³/₄ ounces Orgeat (Almond) syrup*
- *¹/₄ ounce Creme de Cacao syrup*
- *Twist of orange peel, for garnish*

Fill a 12-ounce glass with ice and add the sparkling water. Stir in the syrups and garnish with the orange twist.

ICE CREAM FLOAT

Italian sodas and cream sodas can easily be transformed into beautiful ice cream floats. Simply float a scoop of vanilla ice cream on top of the soda. Fruit-flavored ice creams and sherbets also make scrumptious additions.

CAFFE NIKKO SODA

- *Ice*
- *8 ounces sparkling water*
- *³/₄ ounce Mandarin Orange syrup*
- *¹/₄ ounce Creme de Cacao syrup*
- *Twist of orange peel, for garnish*

Fill a 12-ounce glass with ice and add the sparkling water. Stir in the syrups and garnish with the orange twist.

HAZELNUT SODA

- *Ice*
- *8 ounces sparkling water*
- *1 ounce Hazelnut syrup*
- *Ground nutmeg, for dusting*

Fill a 12-ounce glass with ice and add the sparkling water. Stir in the syrup and dust with the nutmeg.

CHERRY-VANILLA SODA

- *Ice*
- *8 ounces sparkling water*
- *$^3/_4$ ounce Cherry syrup*
- *$^1/_4$ ounce Vanilla syrup*
- *1 Bing cherry, for garnish*
- *Sprig of mint, for garnish*

Fill a 12-ounce glass with ice and add the sparkling water. Stir in the syrups. Garnish with the cherry and the mint.

TAMARINDO TWISTER

- *Ice*
- *8 ounces sparkling water*
- *$^3/_4$ ounce Tamarindo syrup*
- *$^1/_4$ ounce Lemon syrup*
- *Twist of lemon peel, for garnish*

Fill a 12-ounce glass with ice and add the sparkling water. Stir in the syrups and garnish with the lemon peel.

Variation: For added sweetness, try mixing with ginger ale instead of sparkling water.

GARNISHING ICED BEVERAGES

Topping off a beverage adds an element of fun. Here's a quick reference of garnishing ideas: twists of citrus peel • lemon or orange zest • ripe Bing cherries • slices of ripe, fresh fruit • fruit skewers • edible flowers (nasturtiums, pansies) • sprigs of mint • flavored whipped cream • peppermint sticks • cinnamon sticks • shaved chocolate • shaved coconut

ICED TEAS

Delicious iced tea is sweet shade on a hot, summer day. For best results, we recommend combining your favorite flavor with a black tea base like Oolong. Add about 1 ounce of syrup to each 8 ounces of water. Flavored ice cubes (page 36) are another nice addition to this refreshing drink.

❖

ICE BERRIES

- Ice
- 8 ounces brewed tea, chilled
- $1/2$ ounce Raspberry syrup
- $1/4$ ounce Strawberry syrup
- $1/4$ ounce Boysenberry syrup
- Skewer of strawberries and raspberries, for garnish

Fill a 12-ounce glass with ice and add the tea. Stir in the syrups and garnish with the skewer.

❖

STRAWBERRY TROPICS

- Ice
- 8 ounces brewed tea, chilled
- $3/4$ ounce Strawberry syrup
- $1/4$ ounce Creme de Banana syrup
- Slice of strawberry, for garnish

Fill a 12-ounce glass with ice and add the tea. Stir in the syrups and garnish with the slice of strawberry.

BLACK CHERRY

- *Ice*
- *8 ounces brewed tea, chilled*
- *$^3/_4$ ounce Cherry syrup*
- *$^1/_4$ ounce Blackberry syrup*
- *1 Bing cherry, for garnish*

Fill a 12-ounce glass with ice and add the tea. Stir in the syrups and garnish with the cherry.

FRUITED ALMOND

- *Ice*
- *8 ounces brewed tea, chilled*
- *$^3/_4$ ounce Cherry syrup*
- *$^1/_4$ ounce Blackberry syrup*
- *$^1/_4$ ounce Orgeat (Almond) syrup*
- *Sprig of mint, for garnish*

Fill a 12-ounce glass with ice and add the tea. Stir in the syrups and garnish with the mint.

LEMON SPLASH

- *Ice*
- *8 ounces brewed tea, chilled*
- *$^3/_4$ ounce Lemon syrup*
- *Splash of Raspberry syrup*
- *Splash of Strawberry syrup*
- *Slice of lemon or a strawberry, for garnish*

Fill a 12-ounce glass with ice and add the tea. Stir in the syrups and garnish with the lemon slice or strawberry.

MANGO CARIBE ICED TEA

- Ice
- 8 ounces brewed tea, chilled
- $^1/_2$ ounce Mango syrup
- $^1/_4$ ounce Blackberry syrup
- $^1/_4$ ounce Apricot syrup
- Slice of mango, for garnish

Fill a 12-ounce glass with ice and add the tea. Stir in the syrups and garnish with the mango slice. (Pictured opposite.)

PEACH MELBA

- Ice
- 8 ounces brewed tea, chilled
- $^3/_4$ ounce Peach syrup
- $^1/_4$ ounce Raspberry syrup
- Sprig of mint, for garnish
- 1 raspberry, for garnish

Fill a 12-ounce glass with ice and add the tea. Stir in the syrups and garnish with the mint and the raspberry.

CITRUS ICE

- Ice
- 8 ounces brewed tea, chilled
- $^3/_4$ ounce Mandarin Orange syrup
- $^1/_4$ ounce Lemon syrup
- Sprig of mint, for garnish
- Slice of orange, for garnish

Fill a 12-ounce glass with ice and add the tea. Stir in the syrups and garnish with a sprig of mint and orange slice.

- *2 quarts cold water*
- *8 to 10 bags strong black tea*
- *6 to 8 ounces Torani syrup*
- *Ice*
- *Sprig of mint, for garnish*

Put water into a large glass container and add the tea bags. Cover and let sit in the sun for a full day. Discard the tea bags. Sweeten the tea with your favorite syrup. Pour over ice and garnish with a sprig of mint. Makes 2 quarts.

SMOOTHIES

*S*moothies are a delicious, healthy way to enjoy fresh fruits. Torani syrups bring out the full flavor of the fruit.

❖

COCO-BANANA SMOOTHIE

SERVES 4

- 2 cups crushed ice
- $^3/_4$ cup plain yogurt
- $^1/_2$ cup low-fat milk
- $^1/_2$ cup Coconut syrup
- 1 ripe banana, sliced
- Creme de Banana flavored whipped cream (page 17), for topping
- Chocolate powder, for dusting

Combine the ice, yogurt, milk, syrup, and banana in a blender and blend until smooth. Pour into 12-ounce glasses. Top each glass with the whipped cream and dust with the chocolate powder.

❖

MANGO SMOOTHIE

SERVES 4

- 2 cups crushed ice
- $^1/_2$ cup plain yogurt
- $^1/_2$ cup low-fat milk
- $^1/_2$ cup mango nectar, chilled
- $^1/_2$ cup Mango syrup
- $^1/_2$ cup peeled and sliced ripe mango
- 4 mango slices, for garnish

Combine the ice, yogurt, milk, nectar, syrup, and mango in a blender and blend until smooth. Pour into 12-ounce glasses and garnish with mango slices.

SUMPTUOUS BERRY

SERVES 4

- *2 cups crushed ice*
- *1/2 cup plain yogurt*
- *1/2 cup low-fat milk*
- *1/2 cup apricot nectar, chilled*
- *1/2 cup Apricot syrup*
- *1/3 cup fresh raspberries*

Combine the ice, yogurt, milk, nectar, syrup, and raspberries in a blender and blend until smooth. Pour into 12-ounce glasses and garnish with additional raspberries.

PEACHED APRICOT

SERVES 4

- *2 cups crushed ice*
- *1/2 cup plain yogurt*
- *1/2 cup low-fat milk*
- *1/2 teaspoon honey*
- *1/4 cup Apricot syrup*
- *2 ripe peaches, peeled and sliced*

Combine the ice, yogurt, milk, honey, syrup, and peaches in a blender and blend until smooth. Pour into 12-ounce glasses.

TRIPLE BERRY

SERVES 4

- *2 cups crushed ice*
- *1/2 cup plain yogurt*
- *1/2 cup low-fat milk*
- *1/4 cup Cherry syrup*
- *1/2 cup Blackberry syrup*
- *1/3 cup fresh raspberries*

Combine the ice, yogurt, milk, syrups, and raspberries in a blender and blend until smooth. Pour into 12-ounce glasses.

BLUEBERRY SMOOTHIE

SERVES 4

- *2 cups crushed ice*
- *1/2 cup plain yogurt*
- *1/2 cup low-fat milk*
- *1/3 cup Blueberry syrup*
- *1/3 cup fresh blueberries*

Combine the ice, yogurt, milk, syrup, and blueberries in a blender and blend until smooth. Pour into 12-ounce glasses.

STRAWBERRY SMOOTHIE

SERVES 4

- *2 cups crushed ice*
- *1/2 cup plain yogurt*
- *1/2 cup low-fat milk*
- *1/2 cup Strawberry syrup*
- *1/3 cup fresh strawberry halves*
- *4 whole strawberries, for garnish*

Combine the ice, yogurt, milk, syrup, and strawberries in a blender and blend until smooth. Pour into 12-ounce glasses. Garnish with the strawberries.

KIWI PLEASER

SERVES 4

- *2 cups crushed ice*
- *1/2 cup plain yogurt*
- *1/2 cup low-fat milk*
- *1/4 cup Kiwi syrup*
- *1/2 cup Melon syrup*
- *1 ripe kiwi, peeled and sliced*
- *4 kiwi slices, for garnish*

Combine the ice, yogurt, milk, syrups, and kiwi in a blender and blend until smooth. Pour into 12-ounce glasses and garnish each with a kiwi slice.

PEACH MELBA

SERVES 4

- *2 cups crushed ice*
- *¹/₂ cup plain yogurt*
- *¹/₂ cup low-fat milk*
- *¹/₂ cup Peach syrup*
- *¹/₂ cup Raspberry syrup*
- *¹/₂ cup fresh raspberries*
- *1 ripe peach, peeled and sliced*
- *Peach-flavored whipped cream (page 17), for topping*

Combine the ice, yogurt, milk, syrups, and fruit in a blender and blend until smooth. Pour into 12-ounce glasses and top with the whipped cream.

SUNNY SUBSTITUTION

For a tangy twist in your smoothie, substitute orange juice for milk. Those interested in nondairy alternatives may also enjoy soy milk in place of milk.

BERRY BANANA

SERVES 4

- *2 cups crushed ice*
- *¹/₂ cup plain yogurt*
- *¹/₂ cup low-fat milk*
- *¹/₂ cup berry nectar, chilled*
- *¹/₂ cup Raspberry syrup*
- *¹/₄ cup fresh raspberries*
- *¹/₃ cup fresh blueberries*
- *¹/₂ cup ripe banana, peeled and sliced*
- *Skewer of raspberries and blueberries, for garnish*

Combine the ice, yogurt, milk, nectar, syrup, and fruit in a blender and blend until smooth. Pour into 12-ounce glasses. Garnish with the skewer of berries.

Peaches 'n' Cream Smoothie

SERVES 4

- 2 cups crushed ice
- 1/2 cup plain yogurt
- 1/2 cup low-fat milk
- 1/3 cup Peach syrup
- 1 tablespoon Vanilla syrup
- 1 ripe peach, peeled and sliced
- 4 peach slices, for garnish

Combine the ice, yogurt, milk, syrups, and peach in a blender and blend until smooth. Pour into 12-ounce glasses and garnish each glass with a peach slice.

Good Morning Smoothie

SERVES 4

- 2 cups crushed ice
- 1/2 cup plain yogurt
- 1/2 cup orange juice
- 1/2 cup Mandarin Orange syrup
- 1/2 cup Strawberry syrup
- 1 tablespoon Pink Grapefruit syrup
- 1/3 cup fresh strawberry halves
- Strawberry-flavored whipped cream (page 17), for topping

Combine the ice, yogurt, juice, syrups, and strawberries in a blender and blend until smooth. Pour into 12-ounce glasses. Top with the whipped cream.

A *granita is a popular shaved-ice beverage served in cafes. In the following pages we've recreated many cafe favorites that are easy to blend at home.*

A combination of crushed ice, juice, fresh fruit, and flavoring syrup, a "freeze" is a great, low-fat way to celebrate an afternoon or hot evening. Serve in a parfait glass and garnish with fresh fruit.

❖

MAUI FREEZE

SERVES 4

- *2 cups crushed ice*
- *1 1/2 cups unsweetened pineapple juice, chilled*
- *1/3 cup Coconut syrup*
- *1/2 cup fresh pineapple chunks*
- *Pineapple wedges or shaved coconut, for garnish*

Combine the ice, juice, syrup, and pineapple chunks in a blender and blend until smooth. Pour into 12-ounce glasses and garnish each glass with a pineapple wedge or shaved coconut.

SERVES 4

- *2 cups crushed ice*
- *1 cup unsweetened pineapple juice, chilled*
- *1/2 cup orange juice, chilled*
- *1/4 cup Pineapple syrup*
- *1 tablespoon Creme de Banana syrup*
- *1/4 cup fresh pineapple chunks*
- *1 ripe banana, peeled and sliced*
- *Pineapple wedges, for garnish*

Combine the ice, juice, syrups, and fruit in a blender and blend until smooth. Pour into 12-ounce glasses and garnish each glass with a pineapple wedge.

ITALIAN ICE

To make your freeze more like an Italian ice or a granita, pour any of these drinks into a shallow baking pan. Place in the freezer for at least 1 hour. Just before serving, scrape the ice into glasses with a spoon.

T R O P I C A L   S T O R M

SERVES 4

- *2 cups crushed ice*
- *1 cup unsweetened pineapple juice, chilled*
- *1/2 cup orange juice, chilled*
- *1/4 cup Strawberry syrup*
- *1 tablespoon Creme de Banana syrup*
- *1/4 cup fresh pineapple chunks*
- *1/4 cup fresh strawberry halves*
- *Strawberry-flavored whipped cream (page 17), for topping*

Combine the ice, juice, syrups, and fruit in a blender and blend until smooth. Pour into 12-ounce glasses, top each with the whipped cream, and hang on!

SERVES 4

- *2 cups crushed ice*
- *1 cup orange juice, chilled*
- *$1/2$ cup berry nectar, chilled*
- *$1/2$ cup Raspberry syrup*
- *$1/4$ cup raspberries*
- *$1/3$ cup fresh blueberries*
- *Skewers of raspberries and blueberries, for garnish*

Combine the ice, juice, nectar, syrups, and berries in a blender and blend until smooth. Pour into 12-ounce glasses and garnish each with a skewer of berries. (Pictured opposite.)

APRICOT BANANA BLUSH

SERVES 4

- *2 cups crushed ice*
- *1 cup orange juice, chilled*
- *$1/2$ cup apricot nectar, chilled*
- *$1/2$ cup Apricot syrup*
- *1 ripe banana, peeled and sliced*
- *Slices of apricot, for garnish*

Combine the ice, juice, nectar, syrup, and banana in a blender and blend until smooth. Pour into 12-ounce glasses and garnish each with an apricot slice.

ISLAND STRAWBERRY FREEZE

SERVES 4

- *2 cups crushed ice*
- *1 cup unsweetened pineapple juice, chilled*
- *1/2 cup orange juice, chilled*
- *1/2 cup Strawberry syrup*
- *1/4 cup fresh strawberry halves*
- *1/2 cup fresh pineapple chunks*
- *Shaved coconut, for garnish*
- *4 whole strawberries, for garnish*

Combine the ice, juice, syrup, strawberry halves, and pineapple in a blender and blend until smooth. Pour into 12-ounce glasses and garnish each with shaved coconut and a strawberry.

SEA BREEZE

SERVES 4

- *2 cups crushed ice*
- *1/2 cup cranberry juice, chilled*
- *1/2 cup pink grapefruit juice, chilled*
- *1/2 cup Cranberry syrup*
- *1/2 cup Pink Grapefruit syrup*
- *1/4 cup frozen cranberries, thawed*
- *4 slices lemon, for garnish*

Combine the ice, juices, syrups, and cranberries in a blender and blend until smooth. Pour into 12-ounce glasses and garnish each with a lemon slice.

SERVES 4

- *2 cups crushed ice*
- *1 cup brewed coffee, cooled*
- *³/₄ cup Almond Roca® syrup*
- *¹/₄ cup Coffee syrup*
- *Coffee flavored whipped cream (page 17), for topping*
- *Crushed Almond Roca® candy, for garnish*

Combine the ice, coffee, and syrups in a blender and blend until smooth. Pour into 12-ounce glasses, top each with the whipped cream, and garnish with the candies.

SALSAS, SAUCES, MARINADES, AND VINAIGRETTES

CARIBBEAN, ASIAN, Latin American, and Pacific Rim —influenced sauces and condiments are naturals for the pure sweet flavors of many Torani syrups. When a marinade, sauce, or dressing recipe calls for something sweet to balance the tartness of vinegar or the intensity of soy sauce or pepper, a syrup will not only do the trick but add a new dimension as well. Raspberry syrup, for example, makes a more vibrant raspberry vinaigrette, while Caramel syrup, paired with tomatoes, chiles, and spices, gives barbecue sauce a distinctive richness.

In addition to my work at Torani, I own a San Francisco catering business. So it was natural for me to take the syrups from the cafe to the kitchen and start exploring. Torani syrups are natural to cook with because they react to heat very predictably. If you reduce them with other liquids, their flavors intensify. They mix beautifully with wines and liqueurs and add a wonderful caramelized quality to chutneys and relishes.

Grilled fresh fish or chicken marinated with Tropical Marinade, or served simply with Melon Salsa and a green salad makes an elegant and refreshing summer menu; or try pork tenderloin with Brandied Peach Glaze for a delicious, sophisticated winter entree. Grilled Chicken Salad with Mango Vinaigrette is a meal in itself—any time of the year.

49

In fact, Torani is a savior in the kitchen when the fruit you need is out of season or isn't quite ripe. In sauces and glazes, Torani syrups provide the flavor of fresh fruit without the need to peel, purée, or strain. For a pineapple sauce or a blackberry glaze, for example, use a flavored syrup in place of the sugar or corn syrup to add sweetness and enhance the flavor at the same time.

Lisa Lucheta

R. Torre & Company

SALSAS

❖

PINEAPPLE SALSA

This is a delicious accompaniment to grilled fish. It also works well with grilled pork or chicken, or simply as a dip for tortilla chips.

MAKES ABOUT 2½ CUPS

- *2 cups peeled, cored, and diced pineapple*
- *¼ cup Pineapple syrup*
- *1 tablespoon rice vinegar*
- *1 tablespoon finely minced scallion*
- *1 jalapeño pepper, finely minced*
- *¼ cup finely diced red bell pepper*
- *Juice of 1 lime*
- *¼ cup chopped cilantro*
- *1 tablespoon chopped mint*

Mix all the ingredients together in a bowl and serve.

Vibrant Mediterranean flavors come together to produce a salsa that's a perfect topping for grilled fish or chicken.

MAKES ABOUT 2 CUPS

- *4 navel oranges, peeled, sectioned, and diced*
- *$1/4$ cup extra virgin olive oil*
- *2 tablespoons Mandarin Orange syrup*
- *1 tablespoon Champagne vinegar or white wine vinegar*
- *$1/3$ cup pitted, oil-cured olives*
- *1 tablespoon capers*
- *2 tablespoons finely minced shallot*
- *1 teaspoon grated orange zest*
- *$1/4$ cup chopped parsley*
- *Pinch of cayenne*
- *Pinch of salt*
- *$1/2$ teaspoon dried oregano*

Mix all the ingredients together in a bowl and serve.

❖

PEACH AND TOMATO SALSA

This salsa is best when made at the height of the peach season. It makes a tasty and unusual topping for a light fish such as halibut or sea bass.

MAKES ABOUT 2½ CUPS

- *1 cup peeled and diced fresh peaches*
- *¼ cup Peach syrup*
- *1 cup seeded and diced ripe tomatoes*
- *2 tablespoons finely minced shallot*
- *2 tablespoons Champagne vinegar or white wine vinegar*
- *2 tablespoons chopped Italian parsley*
- *Pinch of cayenne*
- *Pinch of salt*

Mix all the ingredients together in a nonreactive bowl and serve.

❖

CLASSIC TOMATO SALSA

The traditional taquería salsa. You'll want to make this for tacos and burritos, or serve it as a dip for chips.

MAKES ABOUT 2½ CUPS

- *2 cups seeded and diced Roma or other thick-walled tomatoes*
- *½ cup diced red onion*
- *1 jalapeño pepper, finely minced*
- *¼ cup Lime syrup*
- *½ teaspoon salt*
- *¼ cup chopped cilantro*
- *1 tablespoon lemon juice*
- *1 small clove garlic, minced*

Mix all the ingredients together in a bowl and serve.

While the melons are an unusual choice for salsa, the combination is mouthwatering. A mix of orange and green melons make it especially colorful. Serve alongside huevos rancheros, with grilled fish or poultry, or in fish tacos.

MAKES ABOUT 3 CUPS

- *2 cups diced (about 1 pound) cantaloupe, honeydew, or crenshaw melon*
- *$^1/_2$ cup diced red onion*
- *$^1/_4$ cup diced sweet red pepper*
- *$^1/_2$ a jalapeño pepper, finely minced*
- *$^1/_4$ cup chopped cilantro*
- *2 tablespoons lime juice*
- *$^1/_4$ cup Melon syrup*
- *$^1/_2$ teaspoon salt*

Mix all the ingredients together in a bowl and serve. (Pictured opposite.)

❖

CARAMEL BARBECUE SAUCE

An instant hit among our food tasters! The combination of syrups and spices makes a dynamite sauce. It is an all-purpose barbecue sauce for grilling ribs, chicken, or your favorite entrée. The chipotle chiles (dried and smoked jalapeños) add a smoky flavor as well as a lot of heat to this sauce. Add more or less according to your taste.

MAKES 1 QUART

- 2 tablespoons olive oil
- 1 large onion, diced
- 3 cloves garlic, chopped
- 1 ounce fresh ginger, coarsely chopped
- 1 can (28 ounces) crushed tomatoes with purée
- 2 dried or canned chipotle chiles, seeded and coarsely chopped
- 1 cup cider vinegar
- $1/2$ cup Caramel syrup
- $1/4$ cup Tamarindo syrup
- 1 tablespoon dry mustard
- 1 teaspoon dried oregano
- 1 teaspoon ground coriander
- $1/2$ teaspoon ground cardamom
- $1/2$ teaspoon ground fennel
- Pinch of ground cloves

Heat the oil in a large saucepan and sauté the onion, garlic, and ginger over low heat for 5 minutes. Add the remaining ingredients. Simmer for 2 hours, stirring frequently. Let the sauce cool, then purée in a blender until smooth.

Roasted lamb or beef tastes delicious with this sauce.

MAKES 1½ CUPS

- 1 cup Black Currant syrup
- 1 cup Zinfandel or other full-bodied red wine
- 2 tablespoons butter
- 2 tablespoons all-purpose flour
- 1 cup beef or rich chicken stock
- ½ teaspoon tomato paste
- Salt and pepper

In a small saucepan, reduce the syrup and wine by half. In another saucepan, melt the butter and whisk in the flour. Cook the roux for 3 to 5 minutes, or until it begins to brown. Slowly whisk in the syrup mixture, then the stock and tomato paste. Simmer for about 30 minutes. Season with salt and pepper to taste.

BRANDIED PEACH GLAZE

Use as a glaze for pork chops, pork tenderloin, or baby back ribs.

MAKES 1½ CUPS

- ½ cup brandy
- 1 cup Peach syrup
- ½ teaspoon balsamic vinegar
- ½ teaspoon curry powder
- Salt and pepper

In a small saucepan, reduce the brandy and syrup by half. The liquid will flame a little as the alcohol burns off. Mix in the vinegar, curry powder, and salt and pepper to taste, and simmer for 5 minutes.

BLACKBERRY SAUCE

This makes a delicious sauce for roast duck or wild game.

MAKES 1½ CUPS

- *½ cup Blackberry syrup*
- *½ pint blackberries*
- *½ cup chopped red onion*
- *1 clove garlic, chopped*
- *1 teaspoon paprika*
- *Pinch of nutmeg*
- *Pinch of salt*

Combine the ingredients in a saucepan and simmer for 20 minutes. Let cool. Purée in a blender and strain.

❖

ASIAN PINEAPPLE DIPPING SAUCE

An all-purpose dipping sauce for egg rolls, wontons, or steamed dumplings.

MAKES ¾ CUP

- *½ cup Pineapple syrup*
- *2 tablespoons soy sauce*
- *2 teaspoons finely minced shallot*
- *1 teaspoon grated gingerroot*
- *2 tablespoons rice wine*
- *½ teaspoon Asian chile paste*

Mix all the ingredients together and serve in individual dipping bowls.

Note: Sake or sherry may be substituted for the rice wine.

Marinades

Lemon Marinade with Rosemary

Rosemary, meaning "dew of the sea," is indigenous to Mediterranean soil. Its dark green, needle-like leaves are highly aromatic, almost woodsy, and lend themselves wonderfully to marinades. This is particularly delicious as a marinade for chicken.

Makes 2 cups

- $^{1}/_{2}$ *cup Lemon syrup*
- $^{1}/_{2}$ *cup white wine*
- $^{1}/_{4}$ *cup olive oil*
- *1 tablespoon grated onion*
- *2 cloves garlic, minced*
- *Several sprigs of fresh rosemary*
- *1 tablespoon grated lemon zest*
- $^{1}/_{2}$ *cup plain yogurt*
- *1 teaspoon paprika*
- *1 teaspoon salt*

Mix all the ingredients together and use as a marinade.

Note: The flavors are best if the meat is marinated for several hours or overnight, then grilled over charcoal. Baste frequently.

When using any acid-based marinade for fish, let the fish remain in the mixture for only 30 to 60 minutes. If it remains longer, the acid will cook the meat.

The flavors of Southeast Asia dominate this spicy marinade. It is particularly good with grilled flank steak but also works well with grilled pork or chicken.

MAKES 1 CUP

- $^1/_2$ cup Coconut syrup
- 2 tablespoons Lemon syrup
- 2 tablespoons Tamarindo syrup
- $^1/_4$ cup peanut oil
- 1 tablespoon Thai fish sauce
- $^1/_4$ cup chopped cilantro
- 1 teaspoon grated gingerroot
- 1 clove garlic, pressed
- 1 teaspoon lime zest
- 1 teaspoon ground cumin
- 1 teaspoon ground coriander
- 1 teaspoon red pepper flakes

Mix all the ingredients together. Reserve a little of the marinade to use as a dipping sauce, particularly if you are making skewered satés.

This marinade may be used for grilling a light fish like a halibut or a meatier fish like swordfish with equally tasty results.

MAKES 1 CUP

- $1/2$ cup Pineapple syrup
- $1/4$ cup Passion Fruit syrup
- 2 tablespoons sherry
- 2 tablespoons soy sauce
- 2 tablespoons peanut oil
- 1 teaspoon grated gingerroot
- 1 teaspoon curry powder
- $1/2$ teaspoon ground cardamom

Mix all the ingredients together. Reserve some of the marinade to drizzle over the fish after it is cooked.

This recipe was developed for grilled lamb kabobs, but is also tasty with grilled beef or pork kabobs.

MAKES 1½ CUPS

- $^3/_4$ cup *Black Currant syrup*
- 2 tablespoons *Lemon syrup*
- $^1/_4$ cup *olive oil*
- $^1/_4$ cup *red wine*
- 2 tablespoons *grated onion*
- 1 clove garlic, minced
- 2 tablespoons *minced fresh dill, or 1 teaspoon dried*
- 2 tablespoons *minced fresh mint*
- 1 teaspoon *dried oregano*
- 1 tablespoon *crumbled bay leaves*
- 1 tablespoon *ground pepper*
- $^1/_2$ *teaspoon salt*

Mix all the ingredients together in a bowl, and refrigerate or use.

This is a fruity, Asian-style marinade that works well with barbecued pork, chicken, or beef.

MAKES 1½ CUPS

- *½ cup Apricot syrup*
- *½ cup Peach syrup*
- *2 tablespoons soy sauce*
- *2 tablespoons sherry*
- *1 tablespoon minced onion*
- *1 teaspoon minced garlic*
- *1 tablespoon minced gingerroot*
- *1 teaspoon paprika*
- *Pinch of cayenne*

Heat the syrups in a small saucepan until reduced by half. Let cool. Add the remaining ingredients and use as a marinade. Reserve some to use as a basting sauce for grilled meats.

VINAIGRETTES

---   ❖   ---

PINK GRAPEFRUIT VINAIGRETTE

It was a thrill to discover the versatility of Torani syrup in tart and tangy applications. You'll want to use the following flavorful vinaigrette over and over again.

MAKES ½ CUP

- *2 tablespoons Pink Grapefruit syrup (see note)*
- *1 teaspoon grated orange zest*
- *2 tablespoons Champagne vinegar or white wine vinegar*
- *1 teaspoon Dijon-style mustard*
- *½ teaspoon salt*
- *Freshly ground pepper to taste*
- *¼ cup extra virgin olive oil*

Combine the syrup, zest, vinegar, mustard, salt, and pepper in a small mixing bowl. Slowly whisk in the olive oil.

Note: Orange, Lemon, or Lime syrup in place of Pink Grapefruit will do equal justice to this recipe.

AVOCADO AND GRAPEFRUIT SALAD WITH PINK GRAPEFRUIT VINAIGRETTE

Juicy red grapefruit, ripe avocado, and the tangy dressing combine to make this a wonderful salad.

SERVES 4

- $1/4$ cup Pink Grapefruit Vinaigrette (recipe precedes)
- 2 ripe Haas avocados, sliced
- 3 ruby red grapefruit, peeled and separated into segments
- $1/2$ pound mixed salad greens

Toss all ingredients together in a bowl and serve at once.

TOASTED WALNUT VINAIGRETTE

Use this vinaigrette whenever a nutty dressing would be appropriate. Salads of baby greens or beets, or any with blue cheese, would be perfect choices, as would Green Bean and Toasted Walnut Salad (page 68).

MAKES $1/2$ CUP

- 1 tablespoon Toasted Walnut syrup
- 1 teaspoon Dijon-style mustard
- 2 tablespoons cider vinegar
- $1/2$ teaspoon salt
- Freshly ground pepper to taste
- 1 teaspoon finely minced shallot
- $1/2$ teaspoon grated lemon zest
- $1/4$ cup extra virgin olive oil

In a small mixing bowl, combine the syrup, mustard, vinegar, salt, pepper, shallot, and zest. Slowly whisk in the olive oil until well combined.

ORANGE, ARUGULA, AND ENDIVE SALAD WITH MANDARIN ORANGE VINAIGRETTE

The slightly bitter taste of endive is mellowed by the flavor of mandarin orange in this colorful salad.

SERVES 4

- ¼ cup Mandarin Orange Vinaigrette (recipe follows)

- ½ pound arugula leaves

- 2 navel oranges, peeled and separated into segments

- 3 heads Belgian endive, leaves separated

Toss all the ingredients together and serve. (Pictured opposite.)

MANDARIN ORANGE VINAIGRETTE

This is a light, citrusy dressing with versatile applications: it contrasts with bitter greens or complements salads made with fruit.

MAKES ½ CUP

- 2 tablespoons Mandarin Orange syrup

- 1 teaspoon grated lemon zest

- 2 tablespoons Champagne vinegar or white wine vinegar

- 1 teaspoon Dijon-style mustard

- ½ teaspoon salt

- Freshly ground pepper to taste

- ¼ cup extra virgin olive oil

Combine the syrup, zest, vinegar, mustard, salt, and pepper in a small mixing bowl. Slowly whisk in the olive oil until well combined.

❖

TOASTING NUTS

Toasting nuts heightens their flavor and adds much to the dish you are preparing. Spread the nuts on a baking sheet and bake in a 350° oven for approximately 10 minutes. Shake the baking sheet once or twice to ensure even coloring and be sure to check them at regular intervals, as they can burn quickly. Nuts should reach a golden brown color.

❖

GREEN BEAN AND TOASTED WALNUT SALAD

Crisp green beans are paired with the roasted flavor of walnuts in this arrangement. Snow peas or sugar snap peas are good substitutes for the green beans, as are almonds or hazelnuts.

❖

Fresh herbs will last longer if stored in the refrigerator. Sprinkle the herbs with water, wrap them with paper towels, and place in a plastic bag. You can also place the cut ends in a jar of cold water.

❖

SERVES 4

- *¹/₄ pound mixed lettuce*
- *1 pound green beans, cooked until crisp, and chilled*
- *¹/₄ cup Toasted Walnut Vinaigrette (recipe precedes)*
- *¹/₄ cup coarsely chopped, toasted walnuts (page 66), for garnish*

Line a platter or four salad plates with the lettuces. Toss the beans with the dressing and place on top of the lettuce. Garnish with the walnuts.

MANGO VINAIGRETTE

The mango in this wonderful dressing evokes the bright colors of the Caribbean.

MAKES 1 CUP

- *¹/₄ cup peeled and diced mango*
- *¹/₂ cup Mango syrup*
- *2 tablespoons balsamic vinegar*
- *¹/₂ teaspoon Dijon-style mustard*
- *¹/₂ teaspoon salt*
- *¹/₄ teaspoon Chinese five-spice powder*
- *¹/₄ cup extra virgin olive oil*

Combine all the ingredients in a blender and blend until smooth.

GRILLED CHICKEN SALAD WITH MANGO VINAIGRETTE

This entrée is one of our favorites. It's great to serve hot off the grill or out of the broiler, or at room temperature for alfresco dining.

SERVES 4

- *4 boneless and skinless chicken breast halves*
- *1 cup Mango Vinaigrette (page 68)*
- *Salt and pepper*
- *$^1/_4$ pound mixed baby lettuces*
- *1 mango, peeled and cut into slices*
- *1 small red bell pepper, cut into julienne strips*
- *1 small yellow bell pepper, cut into julienne strips*
- *$^1/_4$ package rice stick noodles (optional)*
- *Peanut oil for deep frying*

Prepare the grill.

Brush the chicken with $^1/_4$ cup of the vinaigrette. Season with salt and pepper and grill until done, about 5 minutes per side.

Toss the greens with 2 tablespoons of the vinaigrette and arrange in the middle of four dinner plates. Arrange the mango and bell peppers around the edge of the plates. Slice the chicken on the diagonal and fan the pieces on top of the lettuce.

Heat peanut oil in a wok or skillet and quickly fry the rice noodles until they are golden. Let drain on paper towels. Drizzle a little vinaigrette over the chicken and serve the remainder on the side. Sprinkle each salad with some fried noodles and serve.

Note: Bell peppers may be roasted for a smokier flavor.

❖

To roast peppers, place over the burner on a gas stove or under the broiler until skins are black and blistery. Place in a paper bag and close for 15 minutes to steam. The skins will then peel off easily.

❖

RASPBERRY VINAIGRETTE

Syrup provides a flavorful twist on this classic fruity dressing.

MAKES ½ CUP

- ¼ cup Raspberry syrup
- ¼ cup rice wine vinegar
- ½ teaspoon Dijon-style mustard
- ¼ teaspoon ground fennel
- ¼ teaspoon ground coriander
- 1 teaspoon finely minced shallot
- ½ teaspoon salt
- Freshly ground pepper
- ¼ cup extra virgin olive oil

In a small saucepan, heat the syrup and vinegar until reduced by half. Let cool. Combine the raspberry mixture with the remaining ingredients in a blender and blend until smooth.

SHRIMP AND BABY SPINACH SALAD WITH RASPBERRY VINAIGRETTE

The Raspberry Vinaigrette lends a heightened pink color and a fruit flavor to the shrimp in this colorful and refreshing salad.

SERVES 4

- ½ pound baby spinach leaves
- ½ cup Raspberry Vinaigrette (recipe precedes)
- 1 pound cooked shrimp
- 2 Japanese cucumbers, or 1 English cucumber, thinly sliced
- 1 pint cherry tomatoes, cut in half

Toss the spinach with ¼ cup of the vinaigrette and arrange in the center of four dinner plates. Toss the shrimp with the remaining ¼ cup vinaigrette and arrange on top of each salad. Scatter the cucumbers and tomatoes around the edge of each plate and serve at once. (Pictured opposite.)

MENUS FOR ENTERTAINING

IN THIS CHAPTER, we have put together some of our favorite Torani recipes in complementary menus: Caribbean-inspired dishes; eclectic cafe grill–style food; breakfast food from English Toffee Waffles to Lemon Currant Scones; and festive holiday fare.

The first time I used Torani syrups I was catering a wedding for 300 people. The mango salsa I made tasted flat; it needed a flavor boost. So I added Torani Mango syrup and that made all the difference. It was a big hit.

I find the syrups are often easier to work with than special ingredients and can save you a trip to the market. In Thai-Style Marinade (page 60), although I used Lemon, Coconut, and Tamarindo syrups instead of lemon grass, coconut milk, and tamarind, I achieved the same richness and complexity. And the syrups often contribute more than flavor to a dish: in the Apple and Chicken Sausage Patties (page 96), Torani Apple syrup adds moisture as well as flavor, giving the chicken patties a consistency close to pork sausage, but without the fat of pork.

One of the things I like best about cooking with Torani syrups is that they are very forgiving. What you taste is what you get, so that you can experiment without taking a lot of risk. If your tongue tells you that a touch of Toasted Walnut

syrup would add an interesting accent to your favorite holiday yams, try it. Your intuition is probably right.

Feel free to mix it up and serve Phyllo-Wrapped Baked Brie with Apricot Chutney at your next cocktail party, or treat the family to Mandarin Orange Sorbet any time.

Ann Rudirf

Chef and Culinary Director,
R. Torre & Company

A CARIBBEAN MENU

The flavors of the Caribbean islands inspire these dishes. Aromatic spices and syrups provide an abundance of flavor without the fat. So put on some Harry Belafonte, find your beach hat in the back of the closet, and invite a few friends over to a Caribbean dinner.

❖

PORK SATÉ

In this Indonesian dish, chicken, beef, or lamb may be substituted for the pork. Serve with Coconut-Macadamia Sauce (page 76).

SERVES 6 AS AN APPETIZER

- ¼ yellow onion
- 2 garlic cloves
- 1 tablespoon minced gingerroot
- 1 tablespoon soy sauce
- Juice of 1 lemon
- 1 tablespoon Tamarindo syrup
- 1 tablespoon Macadamia Nut syrup
- 2 tablespoons Coconut syrup
- 1 teaspoon ground cumin
- 1 teaspoon ground coriander
- 1 pound lean pork, thinly sliced

Combine all of the ingredients except the pork in a blender and blend until smooth. Skewer the pork and let stand in the marinade for 1 hour. Grill over charcoal or broil for 3 to 4 minutes.

❖

Saté, or satay, is a favorite Indonesian cooking style. Pieces of meat, fish, or poultry are marinated, skewered, and grilled, and often served with a spicy peanut sauce. Satés are featured as appetizers on many American menus.

❖

COCONUT-MACADAMIA SAUCE

Serve this sauce with skewered meat satés.

MAKES 2 CUPS

- $1/2$ cup Coconut syrup
- $1/4$ cup Macadamia Nut syrup
- 1 tablespoon Tamarindo syrup
- 1 teaspoon lemon zest
- Cayenne to taste
- $1/2$ teaspoon salt
- $1/2$ pound roasted peanuts, ground
- $1/2$ yellow onion, finely chopped
- $1 1/2$ cups evaporated milk
- $1/2$ a jalapeño pepper, minced
- 1 clove garlic, minced

Combine all of the ingredients in a saucepan and simmer for 15 minutes.

The "jerked" style of cooking, meat marinated in a spicy chile mixture, originated in Jamaica. Serve with Mango Chutney (page 78).

SERVES 6

- 1 tablespoon ground allspice
- 1 tablespoon ground coriander
- 1 teaspoon ground cinnamon
- $1/2$ teaspoon salt
- 4 scallions, finely chopped
- 2 cloves garlic, pressed
- $1/4$ cup olive oil
- $1/2$ teaspoon ground nutmeg
- $1/2$ teaspoon cayenne
- 1 teaspoon chile powder
- $1/2$ teaspoon pepper
- $1/4$ cup Tamarindo syrup
- $1/4$ cup red wine
- 6 boneless and skinless chicken breast halves

Mix all of the ingredients together except the chicken. Rub over meat and let sit several hours or overnight. Grill over hot coals or broil, turning frequently until fully cooked. (Pictured page 79.)

Use this as a condiment for grilled pork or chicken, spread on a wheel of Brie cheese, or as part of an East Indian banquet.

MAKES 1½ CUPS

- *2 large, semi-ripe mangoes, peeled and diced*
- *1 cup cider vinegar*
- *1 cup Mango syrup*
- *1 clove garlic, pressed*
- *½ teaspoon salt*
- *½ cup raisins*
- *¼ teaspoon ground allspice*
- *½ teaspoon ground cumin*
- *½ teaspoon ground ginger*
- *½ teaspoon mustard seeds*
- *½ a jalapeño pepper, minced*
- *½ cup crystallized ginger*

Combine all of the ingredients in a saucepan. Bring to a boil, then simmer about 1 hour, or until thickened. (Pictured opposite.)

Delicious served with Banana Jam (recipe follows).

SERVES 6 AS A SIDE DISH

- 2 cups peeled and grated garnet or jewel yam
- 1 cup peeled and grated russet potato
- 1 egg
- 1 teaspoon curry powder
- 2 scallions, finely minced
- 1 tablespoon minced parsley
- 1 tablespoon all-purpose flour
- Salt and pepper to taste
- Vegetable oil for frying

Blanch the yam and potato in boiling water for 1 minute. Drain well. Mix with the remaining ingredients except the oil.

Pour oil into a heavy skillet to a depth of $\frac{1}{8}$ inch and heat over medium heat. Drop the batter by table-spoons into the skillet and flatten with a spatula. Fry until crisp, about 4 minutes per side. Serve immediately. (Pictured page 79.)

BANANA JAM

While we've paired this with savory yam pancakes for this menu, please use it on pancakes or toast for breakfast, or on ice cream with hot fudge and nuts as a midnight snack.

MAKES 1½ CUPS

- 6 bananas
- Juice of 2 limes
- 1 cup water
- 3 cups sugar
- 1 tablespoon Vanilla syrup
- 2 tablespoons Creme de Banana syrup

Cut the bananas into ¼-inch slices and toss with the lime juice. Bring the water and sugar to a boil, stirring to dissolve the sugar. Add the bananas and cook 20 to 25 minutes, or until thick.

Remove from the heat and stir in the syrups. (Pictured page 79.)

RED BEANS AND RICE
WITH COCONUT

This makes a simple and tasty side dish for any barbecue menu.

SERVES 6

- 1 cup dried red kidney beans, soaked overnight
- 1 cup long grain rice
- 1 clove garlic, minced
- 1 stick cinnamon
- $\frac{1}{2}$ teaspoon salt
- $\frac{1}{2}$ tablespoon butter
- 1 ounce Coconut syrup
- 1 small onion, chopped
- 1 bay leaf
- 1 small sprig thyme, or $\frac{1}{4}$ teaspoon dried
- Pepper to taste

Drain the beans and cover with 8 cups of cold water. Bring to a boil in a large pot, then simmer for an hour, or until cooked. Mix in the remaining ingredients, adding more water if too dry. Simmer for 20 minutes.

Cover and simmer for another 10 minutes. Remove the pot from the heat and let it sit, covered, for 10 minutes. Fluff with a fork and serve.

MANDARIN ORANGE SORBET

After juicing the oranges you may clean the pulp from each half and use as serving cups.

SERVES 6

- *4 cups fresh orange juice*
- *1 cup Mandarin Orange syrup*

Mix the juice and syrup and freeze in an ice cream maker according to the manufacturer's directions. For refrigerator freezing, place in a shallow pan and allow liquid to freeze. Remove to blender or food processor and blend until smooth.

Food for friends. . .is the essence of cooking.

—BARBARA KAFKA

PINEAPPLE GINGER BEER

It's worth shopping around to locate Jamaican Ginger Beer for its intense ginger flavor. In a pinch, substitute your favorite ginger ale.

MAKES 1 SERVING

- *1 (12-ounce) bottle Jamaican Ginger Beer*
- *2 to 4 tablespoons Pineapple syrup*

Stir together the Ginger Beer and the syrup and serve over ice.

A Cafe Grill Menu

We've adapted this cafe grill menu for summer gatherings, outdoor barbecues, or cool evenings. Add flavor and flair to your occasion with a combination of grilled fish, fresh vegetables, and seasonal fruits. Fire up the grill!

❖

Mango Salsa

Native to Southeast Asia, mangoes are dense and juicy and provide a refreshing component in many foods. Fruit salsas are unsurpassed for their freshness and flavor. Try them with a variety of dishes, especially grilled salmon, tuna, or swordfish.

Makes 2 cups

- $1/4$ cup Mango syrup
- 2 ripe mangoes, peeled and diced
- $1/4$ cup minced red onion
- 1 or 2 jalapeño peppers, finely chopped
- $1/4$ cup chopped cilantro
- 1 teaspoon grated lime zest (1 lime)
- 1 teaspoon grated gingerroot
- 2 tablespoons lime juice (juice of 1 lime)
- $1/2$ teaspoon salt

Toss all of the ingredients together in a nonreactive bowl and serve. Serve with Grilled Salmon with Pineapple Marinade (page 86.)

We hope to demystify paté-making with this easy, great tasting recipe. Serve with Black Currant Mustard (page 88).

- ¹/₂ *cup chopped dried apricots*
- ³/₄ *cup Apricot syrup*
- *1 tablespoon Cognac*
- *1 cup minced yellow onion*
- *4 tablespoons butter*
- *2 cloves garlic, minced*
- *1¹/₂ pounds ground pork*
- *1 teaspoon dried thyme*
- *1 teaspoon dried oregano*
- *1 teaspoon ground fennel*
- *1 teaspoon coarsely ground pepper*
- *1 teaspoon salt*
- ¹/₄ *cup shelled pistachio nuts*

Soak the apricots in the syrup and Cognac for 30 minutes. Preheat the oven to 375°.

Sauté the onions in the butter until they're soft, about 5 minutes. Add the garlic and sauté for 30 seconds more. Combine the onion mixture, apricot mixture, and the remaining ingredients and place in an 8¹/₂ by 4¹/₂ by 2¹/₂-inch ungreased loaf pan. Cover with foil and place in a larger pan. Fill the pan with hot water to the midpoint of the loaf pan and bake in a water bath for 45 minutes. Remove from the oven and let cool.

Place a weight on top of the loaf and refrigerate overnight. Unmold, trim, and slice.

GRILLED SALMON WITH PINEAPPLE MARINADE

This entrée may be served hot or cold, and works equally well with Ahi tuna or swordfish. Serve with Mango Salsa (page 84).

SERVES 4

Pineapple Marinade

- $1/4$ cup Pineapple syrup
- 1 tablespoon soy sauce
- 1 teaspoon grated gingerroot
- 1 small clove garlic, pressed
- 2 tablespoons rice wine, sherry, or sake
- 4 salmon fillets, about 6 ounces each

Note: Attention must be paid to the cooking of this tender, sweet fish. The coals should be burned rather low before placing the salmon on the grill. If the fire sizzles too hot, spray a mist of water on the coals. To test for doneness, "push" on the fish at its middle. The fish is cooked when it gently flakes away from your finger. (Pictured opposite.)

Combine the marinade ingredients. Coat the salmon with the marinade and let sit for 30 minutes.

Grill the salmon until done to your liking, quite pink in the middle, California-style, or more well done if you prefer.

BLACK CURRANT MUSTARD

You can use this fruit-flavored mustard on sandwiches or in salad dressings.

MAKES 1 CUP

- *¹/₂ cup Black Currant syrup*
- *¹/₂ cup whole-grain mustard*

In a small saucepan, simmer the Black Currant syrup until reduced by half. Add to the mustard and mix well.

SUGAR SNAP PEAS WITH MANDARIN ORANGE–SESAME GLAZE

Mandarin Orange syrup provides a flavorful accompaniment to crisp snap peas, complementing the freshness of the vegetable. Be sure to cook the peas al dente.

SERVES 4

- *¹/₄ cup Mandarin Orange syrup*
- *¹/₄ cup rice vinegar*
- *Few drops toasted sesame oil*
- *1 pound sugar snap peas*
- *2 tablespoons toasted sesame seeds*

In a small saucepan, simmer the Mandarin Orange syrup and vinegar until reduced by half. Remove from the heat and add the sesame oil.

Cook the snap peas in boiling, salted water until crisp but tender. Toss with the glaze and top with sesame seeds. (Pictured page 87.)

LEMON BASMATI RICE

Basmati is an aromatic rice from India and Pakistan. Its name means "queen of fragrance." We add a tangy twist to this nutritious staple.

SERVES 4

- ¼ cup Lemon syrup
- 2 cups water
- 1 teaspoon salt
- 1 cup basmati rice
- 1 tablespoon chopped parsley
- 1 teaspoon grated lemon zest

Bring the syrup and water to a boil in a medium saucepan. Add the salt and rice. Simmer over low heat, covered, for 20 minutes. Remove from the heat and let sit for 5 minutes. Add the parsley and lemon zest and fluff with a fork.

Imported rice should always be rinsed before use. Perfectly cooked rice is attained by measuring the rice and the liquids accurately, by not stirring the rice while it's cooking, and by preparing the rice shortly before serving.

MIXED BERRY SHORTCAKES AND ORGEAT (ALMOND) WHIPPED CREAM

This colorful dessert would be equally welcome at a seated dinner or a backyard barbecue.

SERVES 12

Berries

- *3 pints mixed berries (strawberries, raspberries, blueberries, and/or blackberries)*
- *1/2 cup Blackberry syrup*

Shortcake

- *2 cups flour*
- *1/2 teaspoon salt*
- *1 tablespoon baking powder*
- *2 tablespoons sugar*
- *8 tablespoons butter, chilled and cut into pieces*
- *3/4 cup heavy cream*

Orgeat Whipped Cream

- *3 cups whipping cream*
- *1/4 cup Orgeat (Almond) syrup*

Preheat the oven to 450°. Slice the strawberries and mix with the rest of the berries and the Blackberry syrup. Set aside.

Mix the flour, salt, baking powder, and sugar in a food processor. Add the butter and pulse until the mixture resembles cornmeal. While pulsing, add all but 1 tablespoon of the cream. Turn out onto a floured surface and press the dough together. Roll out to a thickness of 1/2 inch and cut circles with a biscuit cutter.

Brush the tops with the remaining cream and bake for 10 to 12 minutes, or until golden brown.

To serve, whip the whipping cream to soft peaks and mix in the Orgeat syrup. Split the biscuits and fill with the berries and the flavored whipped cream.

A BREAKFAST MENU

We discovered that our syrups bring excitement to the breakfast table, too. We think you'll be delighted with the range and unexpected flavor of these delicious breakfast dishes.

❖

LEMON MELON SALAD WITH GINGER AND MINT

Lemon, ginger, and mint combine to make this wonderfully refreshing fruit salad. Use an assortment of seasonal melons.

SERVES 4

- 2 cups Lemon syrup
- 4 ounces gingerroot, peeled and sliced
- 4 cups melon balls
- 1/4 cup chopped fresh mint, for garnish

Place the Lemon syrup and sliced ginger in a saucepan and bring to a boil. Remove from heat and let cool. Refrigerate for 30 minutes.

Strain the syrup and pour over the melon balls. Cover and return to refrigerator to chill for at least 1 hour. Serve topped with the chopped mint. (Pictured page 94.)

ALMOND AND MIXED FRUIT SALAD

The combination of deep red and purple fruits makes a nice presentation.

SERVES 4

- 1 cup pitted Bing cherries
- 1 cup pitted, sliced plums
- 1 cup seedless red grapes
- 1/2 pint blackberries
- 1/4 cup slivered almonds
- 1/4 cup Orgeat (Almond) syrup

In a salad bowl, toss all of the ingredients together and chill.

FRESH BERRY COMPOTE

This compote may be served warm or at room temperature. It is also wonderful served over vanilla ice cream.

MAKES 1 CUP

- 1 pint blueberries, rinsed
- 1/4 cup Blueberry syrup
- 1/2 pint raspberries

In a small saucepan, heat one third of the blueberries with the syrup for about 5 minutes. Let cool for a few minutes. Mix with the remaining blueberries and raspberries.

Serve this waffle warm with Fresh Berry Compote (page 92). The addition of English Toffee gives these waffles such a buttery, syrupy flavor that they're delicious without any topping at all.

- 2 cups flour
- 1 tablespoon baking powder
- 1 teaspoon salt
- 2 eggs, separated
- 1 1/2 cups milk
- 1/2 cup English Toffee syrup
- 6 tablespoons butter, melted

Preheat a waffle iron.

Sift the flour, baking powder, and salt together. Combine the egg yolks, milk, syrup, and butter and whisk into the flour mixture just until smooth. Beat the egg whites to soft peaks and fold into the batter.

Pour the batter into the waffle iron and cook according to the manufacturer's directions. (Pictured page 94.)

CRANBERRY-ORANGE MUFFINS

These muffins are tart and sweet at the same time. They would be perfect on a Thanksgiving buffet table.

MAKES 12 MUFFINS

- $1/_2$ cup dried cranberries
- $1/_2$ cup Cranberry syrup
- $1 1/_2$ cups flour
- $1 1/_2$ teaspoons baking powder
- 1 teaspoon baking soda
- Pinch of salt
- 8 tablespoons butter, melted
- 1 egg, lightly beaten
- 1 teaspoon grated orange zest
- $1/_2$ cup buttermilk

Soak the cranberries in the syrup for 30 minutes. Preheat the oven to 350° and line muffin tins with paper.

Sift the flour with the baking powder, baking soda, and salt into a mixing bowl and make a well in the center. Combine the cranberry mixture with the butter, egg, zest, and buttermilk. Pour the liquid mixture into the well of dry ingredients and stir just until combined. Spoon into muffin tins and bake for 20 minutes, or until a toothpick stuck in the center comes out clean.

APPLE AND CHICKEN SAUSAGE PATTIES

Our tasters went wild over these. The apples keep the sausage patties moist without the fat and the syrup helps the patties to caramelize and brown beautifully.

SERVES 4

- 1¼ pound ground chicken or turkey
- 1 cup peeled and finely diced Granny Smith apples
- ½ cup Apple syrup
- ½ cup finely minced scallions
- 1 teaspoon salt
- ½ teaspoon fennel seeds, crushed
- ½ teaspoon cumin seeds, crushed
- 1 to 2 pinches of ground nutmeg
- Pinch of cayenne
- Butter for frying

Mix all of the ingredients except the butter until well combined. Cover and refrigerate for several hours or overnight. Shape into 8 patties and fry in some butter until browned on both sides and cooked through, about 3 or 4 minutes per side.

Note: With any ground meat or sausage mixture, it's a good idea to cook just a little bit first to taste it and then adjust for seasoning.

These flaky scones are best served fresh and warm from the oven.

MAKES 8 SCONES

- *2 cups flour*
- *2 teaspoons baking powder*
- *$1/4$ teaspoon salt*
- *1 teaspoon grated orange zest*
- *4 tablespoons butter, chilled and cut into pieces*
- *$1/4$ cup currants*
- *1 egg, lightly beaten*
- *$1/4$ cup Black Currant syrup*
- *2 tablespoons heavy cream*
- *2 tablespoons Mandarin Orange syrup*

Preheat the oven to 425°. In a food processor, mix the flour, baking powder, salt, and zest. Add the butter and pulse to mix. Add the currants and pulse again. Mix the egg with the Black Currant syrup and the cream in a separate bowl. With the motor running, pour the egg mixture into the food processor and mix just until it starts to form a dough.

Turn out the dough onto a floured surface and pat into a circle. Cut into wedges and bake for 12 to 15 minutes, or until golden brown. Transfer to a rack to cool and brush the tops with Mandarin Orange syrup.

We found this menu so irresistible that, when we were testing it, we made up the theme of "Christmas in August" as our excuse to enjoy it sans Santa.

❖

And the tree twinkled, and all our hearts were full of true happiness, even if some of our livers were in protest of the seasonal flood of delicious generous bakings and roastings.

—M. F. K. FISHER

❖

❖

PHYLLO-WRAPPED BAKED BRIE WITH APRICOT CHUTNEY

A great dish for entertaining. Place on a large round platter and decorate like a wreath with fresh fruit and nuts. Serve with baguettes and apples.

SERVES 12

Chutney

- ¹/₂ *pound dried apricots, coarsely chopped (see note)*
- *1 cup peeled and diced apples*
- ¹/₄ *cup raisins*
- ¹/₂ *cup diced red onion*
- *2 cloves garlic, minced*
- *1 tablespoon minced gingerroot*
- ¹/₂ *jalapeño pepper, minced*
- *1 cup Apricot syrup*
- ³/₄ *cup apple cider vinegar*
- *1 teaspoon ground coriander*
- *2 teaspoons mustard seeds*
- *1 teaspoon salt*
- *Cayenne to taste*

Combine all the chutney ingredients in a heavy saucepan and bring to a boil. Reduce the heat and simmer for 30 minutes, stirring occasionally. The mixture should have reduced and thickened. Let cool, cover, and refrigerate.

Preheat the oven to 350°. Line a baking sheet with parchment paper.

Pastry

- *8 sheets packaged frozen phyllo dough, thawed*
- *1 cup butter, melted*
- *1 whole wheel Brie, about 2$\frac{1}{2}$ pounds*

Place a sheet of phyllo on the parchment and brush it lightly with butter. Place a second sheet horizontally across the center of the first and brush it with butter.

Place a third sheet diagonally over the stack and brush it with butter. Place a fourth sheet on the stack, laying it on the opposite diagonal so that the third and fourth sheets form an X. Brush the fourth sheet lightly with butter. Place the Brie on top and spread chutney over the Brie. Bring the phyllo sheets up and over the edge of the cheese.

Cover the top of the wheel with the remaining 4 sheets of phyllo, each placed in same pattern as above, and brushed with butter. Fold the ends of the pastry under the bottom of the Brie and bake for 20 to 30 minutes, or until brown. Allow to sit for at least 30 minutes before slicing.

Note: Use the moist-pack variety of apricots, if possible.

Use this spiced peach glaze for other roasted poultry, such as duck, goose, or game hens. The stuffing may be prepared separately and baked as a side dish.

SERVES 12

Stuffing

- *1 cup dried cherries*
- *1 cup Apple syrup*
- *4 tablespoons butter*
- *2 cups chopped celery*
- *2 cups chopped onion*
- *1 cup peeled and chopped apples*
- *1 pound sweet Italian sausage, removed from casings*
- *8 cups day-old bread cubes*
- *2 tablespoons chopped fresh sage leaves, or 2 teaspoons dried*
- *1 teaspoon dried oregano*
- *1 cup chicken stock*
- *Salt and pepper to taste*

To prepare the stuffing, soak the cherries in the syrup for at least 30 minutes.

Heat the butter in a large sauté pan and sauté the celery and onion until soft. Add the apples and transfer to a bowl.

In the same pan sauté the sausage for about 5 minutes, breaking it up while it cooks. Transfer the sausage to the bowl with the celery and onions. Add cherries with syrup and the remaining ingredients.

Turkey

- *1 turkey (15 to 20 pounds), rinsed and dried*
- *8 tablespoons butter, melted*

Glaze

- *1 cup Peach syrup*
- *1 teaspoon ground cardamom*
- *1 teaspoon ground ginger*
- *1 teaspoon dry mustard*
- *$1/2$ teaspoon ground nutmeg*
- *$1/2$ teaspoon paprika*
- *Pinch of saffron threads (optional)*
- *Pinch of cayenne*

To prepare the turkey, preheat the oven to 325°. Loosely stuff the turkey's cavities with the stuffing and truss. (Bake any remaining stuffing separately in a casserole dish.) Roast the turkey on a rack for $3^{1}/_{2}$ hours, basting with the butter every 20 minutes. Make a tent with foil to cover the turkey if it is browning too quickly.

Mix all of the glaze ingredients together and baste the turkey with the glaze every 15 minutes until turkey is done, another hour or so. (The internal temperature of the turkey should be 175°.)

Transfer the bird to a serving platter and make a tent with foil to keep the turkey warm. To make a delicious gravy, pour out the pan drippings, scraping the pan to remove any browned bits. Remove some or all of the fat if you like. Shake $1/4$ cup of flour with $1/2$ cup of water in a small jar to mix. Heat the drippings and the flour mixture together in a small saucepan and stir until thickened. (Pictured page 102.)

SWEET-AND-SOUR RED CABBAGE

Boysenberry syrup helps keep the cabbage red while adding fruit flavor.

SERVES 12

- *4 tablespoons butter*
- *2 cups thinly sliced red onion*
- *1 cup peeled and thinly sliced Granny Smith apples*
- *1 head red cabbage (2 to 3 pounds), shredded into $^1/_4$-inch pieces*
- *$^1/_4$ cup red wine vinegar*
- *$^1/_4$ cup red wine*
- *$^1/_2$ cup chicken stock or broth*
- *$^1/_2$ cup Boysenberry syrup*
- *$^1/_2$ teaspoon salt*

In a medium sauté pan, melt the butter and add the onions and apples. Cook for 2 to 3 minutes. Add the remaining ingredients, stirring to coat. Cover and simmer for 30 to 45 minutes, stirring occasionally. Serve hot.

CRANBERRY-CURRANT RELISH

Orange zest, red wine and cinnamon combine to evoke the flavors and aromas of the holidays in this easy to prepare side dish.

MAKES 2 CUPS

- *1 pound cranberries, washed*
- *$^1/_2$ cup currants*
- *1 tablespoon slivered orange zest*
- *$^3/_4$ cup Cranberry syrup*
- *$^1/_2$ cup red wine*
- *$^1/_2$ stick cinnamon*
- *Pinch of salt*

Chop one third of the cranberries in a food processor, then pour them into a medium saucepan. Add the remaining ingredients and simmer for 30 minutes. Let cool and serve with holiday meats. (Pictured opposite.)

GLAZED BRUSSELS SPROUTS WITH TOASTED HAZELNUTS

Even non-lovers of brussels sprouts will go for this dish, where the vegetable is cooked in a mixture of orange, herbs, and hazelnuts.

SERVES 12

- 4 pounds fresh brussels sprouts, outer leaves removed
- 8 tablespoons butter
- 1 cup sliced shallots
- 1 cup Hazelnut syrup
- $1/4$ cup slivered orange zest
- 1 tablespoon dried thyme
- $1/2$ cup toasted and chopped hazelnuts

Preheat the oven to 350°. Lightly butter a casserole dish.

Cut an X into the root end of each brussels sprout. Blanch the sprouts in boiling, salted water for 5 minutes. Drain and refresh in ice water.

Melt the butter in a sauté pan and cook the shallots for a few minutes, until soft. Add the brussels sprouts and the syrup and cook over medium heat until well glazed, about 3 to 5 minutes. Remove from the heat, add the zest, thyme, and nuts, and bake in the casserole dish for 15 minutes, or until tender and heated through.

BAKED PRALINE YAMS
WITH PECAN STREUSEL TOPPING

This southern-style rendering of holiday yams tastes almost like dessert.

SERVES 12

Praline Yams

- *6 medium-sized yams, peeled and sliced ¼-inch thick*
- *1 teaspoon salt*
- *4 tablespoons butter*
- *½ cup Praline syrup*

Streusel Topping

- *½ cup pecan pieces*
- *¼ cup flour*
- *¼ cup brown sugar*
- *¼ cup Praline syrup*
- *2 tablespoons butter, chilled and cut into small pieces*
- *½ teaspoon ground cinnamon*

Preheat the oven to 375°. Butter a casserole dish and layer the yam slices, sprinkling them with salt as you go. Dot the top with butter and pour syrup over. Cover and bake for 30 minutes, basting occasionally.

Mix the streusel topping ingredients together and scatter over the casserole. Bake, uncovered, for another 30 minutes.

We've combined two holiday pie favorites and topped them with your choice of Torani flavored whipped cream.

- One 9-inch deep-dish frozen pastry crust (or see page 115)

Filling

- 3 eggs, lightly beaten
- 1 cup Praline syrup
- 3/4 cup evaporated milk
- 1/2 cup pumpkin purée
- 1 teaspoon ground ginger
- 1 teaspoon ground cinnamon
- 1/4 teaspoon ground nutmeg
- Pinch of ground cardamom
- Pinch of ground allspice
- Pinch of salt

Topping

- 1 cup pecan halves
- 1 tablespoon Praline syrup

Flavored Whipped Cream

- 1 cup whipping cream
- 3 tablespoons Torani syrup (Praline, Vanilla, or Caramel are good choices)

Preheat the oven to 375°.

Prebake the pastry crust until just set, about 8 to 10 minutes. (You may have to poke the air bubbles with a knife as it cooks.) Transfer the crust to a wire rack to cool. Leave the oven on.

Combine the filling ingredients and mix well. Pour into the crust and bake for 40 minutes.

Arrange the pecan halves on top of the pie. Brush with the Praline syrup and bake for another 5 to 10 minutes, or until a knife inserted in the center comes out clean.

Whip the cream with the syrup of your choice until soft peaks are formed. Serve the pie warm or at room temperature with the flavored whipped cream.

In this recipe, we pair a traditional Italian dessert with cheesecake to produce a sensational, creamy, holiday treat.

SERVES 6 TO 8

C h e e s e c a k e

- *1 (8-ounce) package cream cheese, at room temperature*
- *$1/2$ cup Italian Eggnog syrup*
- *$1/3$ cup sour cream*
- *2 large eggs*
- *1 prepared graham cracker crust*

T o p p i n g

- *$1/2$ cup sour cream*
- *4 tablespoons Italian Eggnog syrup*
- *$1/2$ cup chilled whipping cream*

Preheat the oven to 350°. Beat the cream cheese until soft. Add the $1/2$ cup of syrup and the $1/3$ cup of sour cream and mix well. Add the eggs, one at a time, mixing just until smooth. Pour into the crust and bake for 30 minutes, or just until set. Transfer to a rack for 10 minutes.

Whisk the remaining $1/2$ cup sour cream with 2 tablespoons of the syrup. Spread over the top of the cheesecake. Chill for 5 hours or overnight.

Just prior to serving, whip the cream to soft peaks with the remaining 2 tablespoons of the syrup. Pipe the whipped cream around the edge of the cheesecake with a pastry bag fitted with a star tip.

DESSERTS

ONE OF MY FAVORITE ways to use Torani is in desserts. Because we make the syrups with pure cane sugar rather than corn syrup, they blend perfectly with other ingredients, and you don't have to worry about the taste changing when the dish is baked or chilled.

Torani syrups are naturals for dessert recipes because they complement or enhance many of the flavors commonly used for desserts—or even recreate them, as in Tiramisu syrup, which forms the basis for a great Tiramisu Cheesecake. As we were developing Torani Almond Roca®, a first-of-its-kind "co-brand," dessert options for this flavor were very much on our minds.

The syrups add flavor without fat to simple pleasures like Raspberry Sorbet as well as to more exotic desserts like Macadamia Nut Crème Brulée.

As you experiment with the syrups, you may find that in some cases you will need to adjust the total amount of liquid in the recipe to compensate for the syrup. In others, the additional liquid can be a bonus. The eighteen dessert recipes here are just the tip of the iceberg. With so many flavors to work with, you can invent a dozen variations on a theme.

Paul T. Lucheta

R. Torre & Company

Tiramisu is a rich, traditional Italian dessert from Venice, which has become a staple on American menus. Made with mascarpone cheese, espresso, marsala, chocolate, and ladyfingers, Tiramisu literally means "pick-me-up." Our nonalcoholic syrup recipe will do just that.

SERVES 6 TO 8

Cheesecake

- *1 (8-ounce) package cream cheese, at room temperature*
- *$\frac{1}{2}$ cup Tiramisu syrup*
- *$\frac{1}{3}$ cup sour cream*
- *2 large eggs*
- *1 prepared graham cracker crust*

Toppings

- *$\frac{1}{2}$ cup sour cream*
- *4 tablespoons Tiramisu syrup*
- *Cocoa, for dusting*
- *$\frac{1}{2}$ cup chilled whipping cream*

Preheat the oven to 350°.

Beat the cream cheese until soft. Add the $\frac{1}{2}$ cup of the Tiramisu syrup and the $\frac{1}{3}$ cup of sour cream and mix well. Add the eggs, one at a time, mixing until smooth. Pour into the crust and bake for 30 minutes, or until set. Transfer to a rack to cool for 10 minutes.

Whisk the remaining $\frac{1}{2}$ cup sour cream with 2 tablespoons of the Tiramisu syrup. Spread over the top of the cheesecake. Chill for 5 hours, or overnight. Just before serving dust the top with cocoa powder.

Whip the cream to soft peaks with the remaining 2 tablespoons of the Tiramisu syrup. Pipe the whipped cream around the edge of the cheesecake with a pastry bag fitted with a star tip.

*Try serving this warm with whipped cream or ice cream or even by itself.
We think it's also a comforting breakfast dish.*

SERVES **8**

- *8 cups diced rhubarb*
- *1 pint basket strawberries, quartered*
- *1 tablespoon orange zest*
- *³/₄ cup Strawberry syrup*
- *¹/₄ cup Mandarin Orange syrup*
- *2 tablespoons cornstarch*
- *³/₄ cup butter, chilled and cut into small pieces*
- *2 cups all-purpose flour*
- *1 cup rolled oats*
- *¹/₂ cup brown sugar*
- *1 teaspoon ground cinnamon*
- *Pinch of salt*

Preheat the oven to 350°. Toss the rhubarb and strawberries with the zest. Mix the syrups together and dissolve the cornstarch into them. Combine the two mixtures well and pour into a 3-quart baking dish. Combine the butter, flour, oats, brown sugar, cinnamon and salt in a bowl and mix with your hands until crumbly. Spread over the fruit mixture and bake for about 45 minutes, or until bubbly and browned.

FRESH FRUIT TART

Fresh, seasonal ingredients make this dessert extra tasty.

SERVES 8

Mandarin Orange Tart Crust

- *1 cup flour*
- *Pinch of salt*
- *¼ teaspoon grated orange zest*
- *8 tablespoons unsalted butter*
- *2 tablespoons Mandarin Orange syrup*

To prepare the crust, combine the flour, salt, zest, and butter in a food processor, pulsing until the mixture resembles cornmeal. With the machine running, add the Mandarin Orange syrup and mix just until the mixture starts to hold together. Wrap in plastic wrap and refrigerate for 30 minutes.

Roll out the dough on a lightly floured surface and line a 9-inch tart pan with the dough. Place in the freezer for 30 minutes.

Preheat the oven to 400°.

Prick the frozen shell and bake for 15 minutes, or until brown. You many have to poke it again with a sharp knife while baking to remove any air bubbles. Transfer to a wire rack to cool.

Vanilla Pastry Cream

- *1 cup milk*
- *¼ cup plus two tablespoons Vanilla syrup*
- *3 egg yolks*
- *1 tablespoon cornstarch*
- *1 tablespoon flour*
- *1 tablespoon butter*
- *1 tablespoon Orgeat (Almond) syrup*

Fruit Topping

- *A combination of colorful fruits and berries in season*
- *2 tablespoons Apricot syrup*

To prepare the pastry cream, heat the milk with the ¼ cup Vanilla syrup to the scalding point. Whisk the egg yolks with the cornstarch and flour and then whisk in a little of the milk mixture. Return this to the remaining milk mixture and cook over medium heat, stirring constantly for 3 to 5 minutes, or until thickened. Remove from the heat, stir in the butter, and transfer to a bowl. Cover with plastic and refrigerate for 30 minutes. Before assembling, whisk in the remaining 2 tablespoons of Vanilla syrup and the Orgeat syrup.

To assemble, spread the pastry cream over the cooled tart crust. Arrange the fruit in a decorative fashion over the pastry cream. Brush with the Apricot syrup. Serve at once. (Pictured page 114.)

AMARETTO AND PEACH PIE

The flavors of almond and peach are a winning combination anytime. This twist on the all-American pie is a perfect example.

- Pie crust pastry for a double crust 9-inch pie (below)
- 4 pounds ripe peaches, peeled and sliced
- $1/4$ cup Amaretto syrup
- 2 tablespoons flour
- 1 egg yolk
- 1 tablespoon milk

Preheat the oven to 400°. Roll out half of the pastry dough and line a 9-inch pie plate. Mix the peaches with the syrup and flour and fill the pie crust with the mixture.

Roll out the other half of the pastry dough and form the top crust over the pie. Beat the egg yolk with the milk and brush this over the top of the crust. Cut several slits in the top of the pastry to allow steam to escape. Bake for 1 hour. Allow to cool for 1 hour before serving.

PIE CRUST PASTRY

MAKES TWO 9-INCH PIE CRUSTS

- $2^{1}/_{2}$ cups flour
- 1 teaspoon salt
- $3/4$ cup chilled solid vegetable shortening
- $1/4$ cup or more of ice water

Mix the flour and the salt together in a mixing bowl. Cut in the shortening with knives or a pastry blender until the mixture resembles coarse meal. Add the water a bit at a time and mix just until the pastry holds together. Wrap in plastic and refrigerate for 30 minutes before rolling.

The Raspberry syrup turns these pears a pretty pink color.

SERVES 4

- *4 firm, ripe Bosc or Bartlett pears*
- *3 cups Raspberry syrup*
- *2 strips lemon zest*
- *2 strips orange zest*
- *$1/2$ small stick cinnamon*
- *Mint leaves and fresh raspberries, for garnish*
- *$1/2$ pint heavy cream, whipped into soft peaks*

Peel the pears with a vegetable peeler, leaving the stems intact. Remove the core from the opposite end with the point of the peeler. Heat the syrup with the zests and cinnamon and add the pears. Simmer for 20 to 30 minutes, or until tender but not mushy.

Remove the pears from the syrup with a slotted spoon and chill. Strain the syrup and chill separately. Serve the pears with some of the syrup poured over. Garnish with the mint leaves, raspberries, and whipped cream.

MARINATED PEACHES WITH ALMOND CRÈME FRAÎCHE AND AMARETTI

This is a very simple yet refreshing dessert. Make sure you purchase the tastiest peaches available.

SERVES 4

- *4 ripe peaches*
- *Ice water*
- *1/2 cup Peach syrup*
- *1/4 teaspoon ground nutmeg*
- *1/2 cup crème fraîche*
- *2 tablespoons Orgeat (Almond) syrup*
- *8 amaretti cookies, crumbled*

Bring a pot of water to a boil. Blanch the peaches for 1 minute, then immediately plunge them into a pot of ice water. Peel and slice the peaches, and arrange them in four shallow dishes. Pour the Peach syrup over and sprinkle with the nutmeg.

Mix the crème fraîche with the Orgeat syrup and place a dollop in the center of each plate. Sprinkle the cookies over all and serve at once.

Mascarpone is a delicious and tart Italian dessert cheese that we combine with flaky pastry and a fruity blueberry topping to produce a truly delicious dessert.

- *Mandarin Orange Tart Crust (page 112)*
- *1 pint blueberries*
- *$1/2$ cup Blueberry syrup*
- *$1/2$ pound mascarpone cheese*
- *$1/4$ cup Vanilla syrup*
- *$1/4$ teaspoon grated lemon zest*
- *$1/4$ cup sour cream*

Prebake the Mandarin Orange Tart Crust as outlined in the recipe.

In a small saucepan cook one half of the blueberries with the Blueberry syrup for 5 to 10 minutes. Let cool. Toss with the remaining blueberries and chill.

Lighten the mascarpone with the Vanilla syrup, stir in the zest and the sour cream, and chill well.

When ready to serve, spread the cheese over the bottom of the tart shell. Spread the blueberries evenly over the cheese and serve at once.

O R A N G E   A L M O N D   C A K E

The almond tree, related to the peach tree, produces a sweet yet bitter nut. We combine almonds with fragrant oranges to make a delicious cake without butter. The use of extra virgin olive oil lends a Mediterranean flavor to this dessert.

B a t t e r

- *Zest of 1 orange, cut into $^1/_8$-inch julienne strips*
- *$^1/_4$ cup Orgeat (Almond) syrup*
- *$^1/_2$ cup flour*
- *$1^1/_2$ teaspoons baking powder*
- *$^3/_4$ cup sugar*
- *$^1/_4$ teaspoon salt*
- *2 eggs, well beaten*
- *$^1/_3$ cup extra virgin olive oil*
- *3 ounces almonds, very finely ground*

T o p p i n g

- *1 cup heavy cream, whipped to soft peaks*
- *Orgeat (Almond) syrup to taste*
- *Candied orange peel*

Preheat the oven to 350°.
Blanch the zest in 1 cup of boiling water for 1 minute. Drain and cover with the Orgeat syrup in a bowl for $^1/_2$ hour.

Sift the flour and baking powder together and set aside.

Gradually beat the sugar, salt, and flour and baking powder mixture into the eggs. Add the orange zest and syrup, olive oil and almonds. Stir until mixed.

Bake in a 9 by 4-inch loaf pan for 40 minutes, or until a toothpick comes out clean. Serve sliced with whipped cream sweetened with Orgeat syrup and topped with candied orange peel.

In the first-ever joint venture in the industry, Torani teamed with Brown and Haley to create an Almond Roca®-flavored syrup. Its rich, chocolate-buttercrunch taste comes through in this dessert inspired by the French. Served in a cappuccino cup, topped with Almond Roca® "foam" and dusted with cocoa or cinnamon, this makes a rich and delicious dessert.

MAKES 4 SERVINGS

- *½ cup Coffee syrup*
- *1 cup heavy cream*
- *½ cup half-and-half*
- *½ cup plus 1 tablespoon Almond Roca® syrup*
- *6 egg yolks, beaten*
- *Cocoa, or ground cinnamon, for dusting*
- *Shaved chocolate*

In a small saucepan, heat the Coffee syrup and reduce by half. Pour into four small cappuccino cups. In another saucepan heat 2 cups of the cream, the half-and-half, and the ½ cup of Almond Roca® syrup. Slowly whisk ¼ cup or more of the cream mixture into the eggs to temper them. Pour them back into the saucepan and cook for 2 to 3 minutes, stirring constantly until thickened. Pour into the cappuccino cups and let cool. Refrigerate, covered, for several hours or overnight.

Whip the remaining ½ cup cream and 1 tablespoon syrup to soft peaks, and spoon over the chilled custards. Dust with cocoa, cinnamon, or shaved chocolate and serve. (Pictured opposite.)

ALMOND ROCA® ICE CREAM PIE

For a cool, summer, make-ahead dessert, try a delicious mix of butter-crunch, almonds, and ice cream.

First Layer

- *1 package almond toast cookies*
- *$1/2$ cup slivered almonds*
- *$1/2$ cup butter or margarine*
- *$1/4$ cup sugar*

Second Layer

- *$1/2$ cup slivered almonds*
- *2 ounces semisweet chocolate pieces, broken*
- *$1/2$ cup crushed butter toffees*
- *2 quarts of ice cream*
- *$1/2$ cup Almond Roca® syrup*

To prepare the bottom layer, preheat the oven to 350° and butter a 9-inch pie plate. Place the cookies, $1/2$ cup almonds, butter or margarine, and sugar into a food processor and process until the mixture resembles the consistency of oatmeal. Reserve $1/4$ cup of the mixture for the topping and pat the rest into the bottom of the pie plate. Bake for 10 to 15 minutes. Let cool.

To prepare the middle layer, place the remaining $1/2$ cup of almonds, chocolate, and toffees in the food processor and blend until the mixture is crumbly. Reserve $1/4$ of the mixture for the topping. Combine the remaining mixture with the ice cream and the syrup by gently mixing them together until just blended. (Over-mixing can cause ice and crystallizing after freezing.) Mound the mixture into the cooled pie crust.

Combine the reserved cookie mixture with the reserved nuts and candy mixture and sprinkle them over the ice cream pie. Place in the freezer until firm.

RASPBERRY-CHOCOLATE MOUSSE

This recipe was developed by Gloria DeMartino of Hamden, Connecticut. It may be prepared ahead of time and is perfect for entertaining.

SERVES 4

- *8 ounces semisweet chocolate*
- *1½ tablespoons confectioners' sugar*
- *3 egg yolks*
- *3½ tablespoons Raspberry syrup*
- *1 cup heavy cream*
- *1 tablespoon Vanilla syrup*

Cut the chocolate into chunks and melt in a double boiler. Add sugar, egg yolks, and Raspberry syrup, and stir to blend. Remove from the heat and let cool.

Whip the cream with the Vanilla syrup to soft peaks. Fold the whipped cream into the chocolate mixture and spoon into four wine or parfait glasses. Chill well and serve.

Vanilla heightens the flavor of chocolate. The Aztecs discovered this centuries ago, flavoring the hot cocoa-based drinks with vanilla.

FRESH STRAWBERRIES WITH STRAWBERRY AND BALSAMIC SAUCE

In Italy fresh strawberries are often served with a fine aged balsamic vinegar and cracked black pepper. We've sweetened it up a little and enhanced the fruit flavor with Torani Strawberry syrup. You'll love the results.

SERVES 4

- *2 pints fresh strawberries, cut into quarters*
- *1 cup Strawberry syrup*
- *³/₄ cup balsamic vinegar*
- *Cracked black pepper, for garnish*
- *Crème fraîche (optional)*

Divide the strawberries into four sherbet or parfait glasses. Heat the syrup with the vinegar in a small saucepan and simmer until reduced by half. Let cool completely, pour over the strawberries and garnish with the cracked pepper and crème fraîche, if desired, and serve. (Pictured opposite.)

RASPBERRY SORBET

This sorbet is intense in both flavor and color—raspberries at their finest!

MAKES 1 QUART

- *2 pints raspberries*
- *$1/_4$ cup fresh orange juice*
- *$1/_4$ cup fresh lemon juice*
- *2 cups Raspberry syrup*

Purée the berries in a blender or food processor with the juices and syrup. Strain to remove seeds. Chill well, then freeze in an ice cream maker according to manufacturer's directions. Transfer to a bowl, cover, and freeze for an hour or more before serving.

Note: See Mandarin Orange Sorbet (page 83) for instruction on refrigerator freezing.

COFFEE GRANITÉ

While a sorbet is stirred while it freezes to create a smooth texture, a granité is frozen without stirring to produce a coarser, icier dessert.

SERVES 4

- *1 cup Coffee syrup*
- *3 cups very strong, brewed black coffee*
- *1 cup whipping cream*
- *2 tablespoons Vanilla syrup*

Mix the Coffee syrup with the coffee and freeze in a flat pan. With a spoon, scrape into fine shavings into chilled parfait glasses. Whip the cream and Vanilla syrup together to soft peaks and place a dollop on each serving. Serve at once.

CHOCOLATE-AMARETTO TORTE

This rich, velvety torte is flavored with amaretto to produce chocolate heaven.

SERVES 8 TO 10

- *6 ounces bittersweet chocolate*
- *10 tablespoons butter*
- *$1/2$ cup plus 2 tablespoons Amaretto syrup*
- *2 tablespoons Creme de Cacao syrup*
- *5 eggs, separated*
- *$1/4$ cup sugar*
- *Pinch of salt*
- *$1/3$ cup cake flour, sifted*
- *2 cups whipping cream*

Preheat the oven to 350°. Butter a 9 by 5 by 3-inch loaf pan and line the bottom with parchment paper.

Melt the chocolate in a double boiler along with the butter, $1/2$ cup of the Amaretto syrup, and the Creme de Cacao syrup. Let cool.

Beat the egg yolks and sugar into ribbons with a mixer. Stir in the chocolate mixture. Whip the egg whites with the salt to soft peaks.

Fold the flour and the egg whites into the chocolate mixture. Pour into the loaf pan and cover with plastic wrap. Place in a slightly larger pan and fill with hot water to 2 inches up the sides of the pan. Cover the whole thing with foil and bake for 40 to 50 minutes, or until a toothpick comes out clean. Remove from the water bath, but let the cake cool in the loaf pan.

Whip the cream with the remaining 2 tablespoons of Amaretto syrup to soft peaks. Invert the cake onto a serving platter and serve with the whipped cream.

Our version adds a nutty flavor to this rich chilled custard with the caramelized topping.

❖

BAVARIAN CREAM

Mix 1 quart of your favorite vanilla pudding recipe with 1 cup of flavoring syrup. (English Toffee, Almond Roca®, Irish Cream, Praline, or Tiramisu are recommended.) Whip 1 pint of heavy cream to soft peaks and fold into pudding for a delicious mock Bavarian Cream.

❖

SERVES 4

- *6 egg yolks*
- *½ cup brown sugar*
- *1 pint heavy cream*
- *Pinch of salt*
- *3 tablespoons Macadamia Nut syrup*
- *¼ cup chopped macadamia nuts*

Preheat the oven to 350°. Mix the yolks with ¼ cup of the brown sugar. Scald the cream over low heat and whisk it into the egg mixture. Add salt and whisk in 2 tablespoons of the syrup. Pour the custard into four small ramekins or soufflé dishes. Place in a baking pan and fill with hot water to the midpoints of the soufflé cups. Bake for 30 minutes, or until the mixture begins to set. (It should gel more as it cools.) Chill in refrigerator for at least 12 hours.

When ready to serve, mix the remaining ½ cup brown sugar, the nuts, and the remaining 1 tablespoon of syrup and distribute evenly on top of each custard. Place under the broiler until the sugar becomes brown and caramelized.

INDEX

All forty-plus flavors of Torani syrups are caffeine-free and alcohol-free, contain no fat, and are low in calories. Available flavors include:

Almond Roca®	Apricot	Boysenberry
Cherry	Coffee	Creme de Menthe
Hazelnut	Lemon	Mango
Peach	Praline	Tiramisu
Amaretto	Black Currant	Butter Rum*
Chocolate Mint	Cranberry	English Toffee
Irish Cream	Lime	Melon
Peppermint*	Raspberry	Toasted Walnut
Anisette	Blackberry	Butterscotch
Cinnamon	Creme de Banana	Grape
Italian Eggnog*	Macadamia Nut	Orgeat (Almond)
Pineapple	Strawberry	Vanilla
Apple	Blueberry	Caramel
Coconut	Creme de Cacao	Grenadine
Kiwi	Mandarin Orange	Passion Fruit
Pink Grapefruit	Tamarindo	

* seasonal flavors

Torani syrups may be found in espresso carts and in fine restaurants and cafes throughout the United States and Canada and overseas. They may be purchased in a variety of sizes in specialty shops and grocery stores. If you would like the location of the retail outlet nearest you, or if you have any questions about the product, please call R. Torre & Company at (800) 775-1925.